Yezhov v

The Truth About Mass Repressions and the So-Called 'Great Terror' in the USSR

By Grover Furr

Erythros Press & Media, LLC   2016

Corrected Edition April 2017

Third Edition, 2018

Yezhov vs Stalin: The Truth About Mass Repressions and the So-Called 'Great Terror' in the USSR

First Edition: 2016

Published by Erythros Press and Media, 2016

PO Box 291994

Kettering, Ohio 45429

media@erythrospress.com

Published and printed with permission of the author, who assumes all responsibility for the content herein.

Furr, Grover C. (Grover Carr)

Yezhov vs Stalin: The Truth About Mass Repressions and the So-Called 'Great Terror' in the USSR / Grover C. Furr; translations by Grover C. Furr

ISBN: 978-0-692-81050-7

250 pp. Includes index.

Table of Contents

Acknowledgements and Dedication

I would like to express my thanks to the dedicated staff of Harry S. Sprague Library, Montclair State University.

I am especially grateful for the invaluable work of the Inter-Library Loan librarians Kevin Prendergast, Arthur Hudson, and Siobhan McCarthy. Without their hard work I simply could not obtain the many hard-to-find books and articles, in many languages, that make my research possible.

My publisher, cover designer, cogent critic, and friend Mike Bessler of Erythros Press and Media, LLC, has given me encouragement, inspiration, and help whenever I needed it, often at late night hours. I could not ask for a better publisher.

Once again my colleague and friend Vladimir L'vovich Bobrov, of Moscow, Russia, has given unstintingly of his time and help to make this book a reality. I cannot do justice to the contribution he has made to this book, as to all my research and our joint research, in the field of history of the Stalin period.

Professor Susana M. Sotillo, Ph.D., my *camerada* and *compañera*, has helped me immeasurably with her patience and affectionate encouragement more than any words of mine can express.

My deepest thanks to all of you.

* * * * *

I dedicate this book to my son Derek James Furr, once a wonderful boy, now a valued friend.

Grover C. Furr
Bloomfield and Montclair, NJ
November 2016

Publisher's Note on Spelling and Transliteration

By and large, transliteration of Russian names and terms presented herein follows a transliteration system utilized by the OCLC database. With regard to the names "Ezhov" and "Ezhovshchina," – which are integral to the volume at hand – we have utilized a scholarly transliteration, save for the noteworthy exception of the title, which utilizes the more commonly accepted spelling of "Yezhov." By using the latter transliteration in the book's title, we hope to make this book easier to locate for Western librarians and researchers who are more familiar with that spelling.

Introduction.

What It Was

On February 25, 1956 Nikita S. Khrushchev delivered his famous "Closed Report" — inaccurately called, in English, "Secret Speech" — to the delegates at the XX Party Congress of the CPSU. Khrushchev attacked Stalin (and Lavrentii Beria) for committing a number of crimes against members of the Party. Khrushchev stated:

> It was determined that of the 139 members and candidates of the party's Central Committee who were elected at the 17th Congress, 98 persons, i.e., 70 per cent, were arrested and shot (mostly in 1937-1938). ... Of 1,966 delegates with either voting or advisory rights, 1,108 persons were arrested on charges of anti-revolutionary crimes, i.e., decidedly more than a majority.

> ... Now, when the cases of some of these so-called "spies" and "saboteurs" were examined, it was found that all their cases were fabricated. Confessions of guilt of many arrested and charged with enemy activity were gained with the help of cruel and inhuman tortures.

Khrushchev claimed that Nikolai Ezhov, the Commissar of the NKVD from August 1936 until November 1938, must have acted under Stalin's orders.

> It is clear that these matters were decided by Stalin, and that without his orders and his sanction Yezhov could not have done this.

At the XXII Party Congress in October 1961 Khrushchev's men attacked Stalin even more strongly. From this point until sometime after Khrushchev was ousted from power in October 1964 many books and articles appeared that amplified and elaborated

Khrushchev's attack against Stalin. However, archival evidence in support of these attacks was not published.

The "Great Terror"

In 1968 British writer Robert Conquest published a book titled *The Great Terror. Stalin's Purge of the Thirties.* Conquest's sources were Khrushchev-era books and articles, and a hodgepodge of other accounts that alleged crimes by Stalin. Conquest cited all this material without source criticism, as though the claims made in it were unproblematically accurate, were "evidence."

To any careful student of history it was obvious from the outset that Conquest's book was without value as an attempt to establish historical truth. But it proved to be of enormous value as anticommunist *propaganda*. Scholars of Soviet history began to use the title of Conquest's book, "the great terror," as a designation for this period of Soviet history.

Between 1987 until the end of the USSR in December 1991, under the auspices of Mikhail Gorbachev, an even more powerful wave of accusations and denunciations of Stalin as a mass murderer poured from Soviet presses, again without archival evidence.

A report prepared for Khrushchev no later than February 18, 1963 and using archival materials stated that in 1937 and 1938 681,692 persons were shot, while the number shot in 1935-1936 was 2347 and the number shot in 1939 and 1940 was 4464. The source was a report sent to Malenkov and Khrushchev on May 5, 1954 prepared by a certain Colonel Pavlov of the MVD and signed by S.N Kruglov, Minister of the MVD. These figures have been confirmed in recent publications by the FSB, the successor to the MVD – NKVD.

In the Soviet Union the period of mass repressions in 1937-1938 was known as the "Ezhovshchina," or "bad time of Ezhov." After Conquest's book Western historians began to call it the "great terror." Since the end of the Soviet Union anticommunist historians from the former Soviet states including Russia have largely adopted this term.

We will use the term "Ezhov's mass repression" for the large-scale executions and imprisonments of roughly July 1937 to November 1938. Although it is good as a Russian term, "Ezhovshchina" conveys no meaning in other languages. The term "great terror" is useful to anticommunists and anti-Stalinists, including Trotskyists, as a term of abuse against the Soviet government led by Stalin. Furthermore, it conveys a falsehood — that the Stalin leadership ruled by "terror" or that "terror" was the outcome of its policies. A number of Western historians, including some who are strongly anticommunist, agree that the term is unsuitable.

The Anti-Stalin Paradigm

The goal of the present book is to identify the causes of the repressions of, and properly locate the responsibility for, this period. Historians of the Soviet Union propose several different explanations. All of them are fundamentally wrong. Simply put, the reason for this failure is that these historians are not in fact trying to discover the causes of the mass repressions. Instead, they are trying to find the explanation that best fits the preconceived historical framework, or paradigm, for this period. I call this the "anti-Stalin paradigm."

The proximate origin of the anti-Stalin paradigm is in the 1930s writings of Leon Trotsky, by then exiled from the USSR. Trotsky depicted Stalin as a monster. But Trotsky did so in service to his own conspiracy. In reality Trotsky was lying about almost everything that concerned Stalin and the USSR. Of course Trotsky had to lie to his followers too, and they believed him, as did a few others.

In his "Secret Speech" of 1956 Nikita Khrushchev took up a number of the same falsehoods that Trotsky had invented, perhaps directly from Trotsky's works. At the XXII Party Congress in 1961 Khrushchev and his men accused Stalin of yet worse crimes. Today we know that Khrushchev was lying in virtually everything he said about Stalin as well as about Lavrentii Beria, who had replaced Nikolai Ezhov as chief (People's Commissar) of the NKVD in November 1938.

From 1962 on Khrushchev sponsored hundreds of articles and books in which Stalin and his associates were accused of yet more crimes. These were taken up by Western anticommunist writers. Among the most notable were Robert Conquest and Stephen F. Cohen. They and many other anticommunist writers in the capitalist world spread Khrushchev's and Trotsky's lies along with lies concocted by Nazi collaborators and other anticommunists of all stripes.

Mikhail Gorbachev sponsored an avalanche of more anti-Stalin writings that outdid that of Khrushchev's last years. These contributed mightily to the ideological dismantling of the Soviet Union. They are perpetuated by today's anticommunist academics.

According to the anti-Stalin paradigm:

> * Stalin was a "dictator." Therefore, he either initiated or could have stopped everything important that occurred. Therefore, whatever happened, happened because he wanted it, or something very like it, to happen. Stalin was always "in control."

> * The alleged conspiracies against the Stalin government were all fabrications. None of them really existed.

> * It follows that the evidence produced in the testimony at the Moscow Trials, and in the interrogations and confession statements that have gradually been published since the end of the USSR in 1991, must be fabrications and so are disregarded.

> * Stalin never wanted democratic elections. The struggle by Stalin and his supporters for contested elections to the soviets (the legislative arm of the Soviet government) was either a sham or intended as a mechanism to get rid of entrenched local leaders whose power Stalin perceived as threatening in some way.

Mainstream historians of the Stalin period in the USSR bind themselves *a priori* to these tenets. They are not questioned. Nor is there any attempt to validate them. These strictures dictate the kinds of explanations and the types of evidence that are deemed acceptable in mainstream historiography. Their purpose is to guarantee that the only historical explanations set forth in mainstream historiography are those that make Stalin and the USSR "look bad." They are convenient to the view of the USSR as "totalitarian," a "dictatorship" ruled by "terror." They reinforce the concept of this period as "the great terror" and are in turn reinforced by this inaccurate term.

These are *disabling* assumptions. Accepting them makes it impossible to understand Soviet history of the Stalin period accurately. But their aim was never to facilitate an accurate account of history. Rather, their purpose is to reinforce an anticommunist, virtually demonized view of Stalin and the USSR, and thereby of the world communist movement of the 20th century. In this book I make no such *a priori* assumptions.

Books about the so-called "great terror" continue to appear. A recent example is *The Great Fear. Stalin's Terror of the 1930s* (Oxford University Press, 2016) by British historian James Harris. Harris is not one of the fire-breathing anti-Stalinists. His tone is moderate and, for the field of Soviet history, relatively objective.

However, in common with all other mainstream academic historians of this period, including the Trotskyist historians, Harris ignores all the evidence long available that proves that the massive executions were not Stalin's doing but the product of Ezhov's conspiracy. This is the only way to "save" what I have called "the anti-Stalin paradigm" of Soviet history – the only paradigm acceptable to mainstream scholarship. Harris endorses the long-disproven story of the German SD plot to frame Marshal Tukhachevskii (169-70), repeats the similarly disproven tale that Kirov's murderer "was almost certainly acting alone" and decides, in the face of all the evidence, that the fears of challenges to the Stalin government were false. (186) As the reader of this book will discover, this is all wrong.

The Need for Objectivity

Everybody has biases. But everybody can learn to be objective in studying any subject, whether it be physics or history. The techniques are basically similar. Objectivity as a scientific method is a practice of "distrust of the self." One can learn to be objective by training oneself to become aware of, to articulate, and then to doubt one's own preconceived ideas. One must be automatically

suspicious of evidence that tends to confirm one's own preconceived ideas, prejudices, and preferences. One must learn to give
an especially generous reading, to search especially hard for, to
lean over backwards to consider, evidence and arguments that
contradict one's own preconceived ideas.

This is simply what every bourgeois detective in every detective
story knows. As Sherlock Holmes said:

> It is a capital mistake to theorize before you have all
> the evidence. It biases the judgment. (Conan Doyle,
> *A Study in Scarlet*)

In other words: keep your mind free of precipitate conclusions. Get
the facts before you form your hypotheses. Be ready to abandon a
hypothesis that does not explain the established facts. Confirmation bias, "the tendency to search for, interpret, favor, and recall
information in a way that confirms one's preexisting beliefs or hypotheses, while giving disproportionately less consideration to
alternative possibilities," is a powerful force, and "the effect is
stronger for emotionally charged issues and for deeply entrenched
beliefs."

If one does not begin one's research with a determined attempt to
be objective, accompanied by definite strategies to minimize one's
own biases, then one cannot and will not discover the truth. Put
colloquially: if you don't start out to look for the truth you will not
stumble across it by accident along the way, and what you do find
will not be the truth.

The Anti-Stalin Paradigm

The need for objectivity and the fallacies that result when this
principle is not observed, are well known. Therefore the real purpose of most research into Soviet history is not to discover the
truth. Instead it is to arrive at politically acceptable conclusions
and to disregard the evidence when that evidence does not support those politically acceptable conclusions. This is the "anti-
Stalin paradigm."

How is it possible that these fallacies are so commonly applied to
Soviet history of the Stalin period by scholars and other educated

persons? I believe this is due to the power of the "anti-Stalin paradigm." Stalin has been so maligned, by so many "experts" and for so long a time that many people believe "where there's smoke, there's fire" — "there must be something to this."

This is all wrong. There is no substitute for evidence. In this study we examine the evidence and draw conclusions from the evidence alone. This is the only rationally defensible way of proceeding, in history as in any other field of scientific investigation.

The Key Questions

Briefly stated, the keystone questions concerning the mass repressions known as the "Ezhovshchina" or "Great Terror" are these:

> 1) Did hundreds of thousands of innocent victims meet their deaths?
>
> 2) Was Stalin responsible for these murders, as is usually claimed?
>
> 3) If — as the evidence demands that we conclude — Stalin was innocent and put a stop to this crime against humanity, how could he and his colleagues have been oblivious to what was happening for so long? Why were Ezhov and his men able to go on killing so many innocent people for over a year?

The present study attempts to answer these questions.

Procedure

The goal of this book is to explain the Ezhov mass repressions of 1937-1938. Two related sets of events are crucial to understanding these mass repressions. The first is Stalin's struggle for electoral democracy and its defeat. The second is the set of interlocking conspiracies involving supporters of Grigorii Zinoviev, of Leon Trotsky, of Nikolai Bukharin, Genrikh Iagoda, Nikolai Ezhov, and many others, called the "Rights"; and of military figures, of which the "Tukhachevskii Affair" is the best known.

We will review the evidence in as objective a manner as possible, and draw our conclusions based on the evidence and on logical interpretations of it. Mainstream historians of the Soviet Union cannot do this because they are bound by the disabling strictures of the "anti-Stalin paradigm." Therefore the final result of our study — the only one that satisfies the evidence now available and that refuses to throw out any of this evidence on *a priori* grounds — is very different from any of the interpretations of mainstream Soviet historians.

Chapter 1. Elections

This chapter outlines Joseph Stalin's attempts, from the early 1930s until 1937, to democratize the government of the Soviet Union.[1]

This story is well known in Russia, where respect for, even admiration of, Stalin is common. However, this story and the facts that sustain it are virtually unknown outside Russia, where the Cold War paradigm of "Stalin as Villain" so controls what is published that the works cited here are still scarcely noted.

This chapter does not simply inform readers of new facts about, and interpretations of, the history of the USSR. Rather, it is an attempt to bring to a non-Russian readership the results of new research, based on Soviet archives, on the Stalin period and Stalin himself. The facts discussed herein will be utterly unacceptable – in fact, will appear outrageous – to those whose political and historical perspectives have been based upon erroneous and ideologically motivated "Cold-War" notions of Soviet "totalitarianism" and "Stalinist terror."

The Khrushchevite interpretation of Stalin as power-hungry dictator, betrayer of Lenin's legacy, was created to fit the needs of the Communist Party's top leadership in the 1950s. But it shows close similarities, and shares many assumptions, with the canonical discourse on Stalin inherited from the Cold War, which served the desire of capitalist elites to argue that communist struggles, or indeed any struggles for working-class power, must inevitably lead to some kind of horror.

It also suits the Trotskyists' need to argue that that the defeat of Trotsky, the "true revolutionary," could only have come at the hand of a dictator who, it is assumed, violated every principle for

---

[1] This chapter is an abbreviated version of "Stalin and the Struggle for Democratic Reform, Part One," where full documentation and longer quotations can be found. See *Cultural Logic*, April 2005. At http://eserver.org/clogic/2005/furr.html

which the revolution had been fought. Khrushchevite, Cold-War anti-communist, and Trotskyist paradigms of Soviet history are similar in their dependence on a virtual demonization of Stalin, his leadership, and the USSR during his time.

During the 1930s the Stalin leadership was concerned not only to promote democracy in the governance of the state, but to foster inner-party and trade-union democracy as well. We will discuss how the struggle for democracy in all three areas – government, trade union, and Party – developed and were ultimately defeated.

This book draws upon primary sources whenever possible. But it relies most heavily upon scholarly works by Russian historians who have access to unpublished or recently-published documents from Soviet archives.

A New Constitution

In December 1936 the Extraordinary 8th Congress of Soviets approved the draft of the new Soviet Constitution. It called for secret ballot and contested elections.

Candidates were to be allowed not only from the Bolshevik Party — called the All-Union Communist Party (Bolshevik) at that time — but from other citizens' groups as well, based on residence, affiliation (such as religious groups), or workplace organizations. This last provision was never put into effect. Contested elections were never held.

The democratic aspects of the Constitution – by "democratic" here we mean "consistent with social-democratic, i.e. capitalist, notions of democracy" — were inserted at the express insistence of Joseph Stalin. Together with his closest supporters in the Politburo of the Bolshevik Party Stalin fought tenaciously to keep these provisions. He, and they, yielded only when confronted by the complete refusal by the Party's Central Committee, and of the panic surrounding the discovery of serious conspiracies, in collaboration with Japanese and German fascism, to overthrow the Soviet government.

In January 1935 the Politburo assigned the task of outlining the contents of a new Constitution to Avel' Enukidze who, some months later, returned with a suggestion for open, uncontested elections. Almost immediately, on January 25, 1935, Stalin expressed his disagreement with Enukidze's proposal, insisting upon secret elections.

Stalin made this disagreement public in a dramatic manner in a March 1936 interview with American newspaper magnate Roy Howard. Stalin declared that the Soviet constitution would guarantee that all voting would be by secret ballot. Voting would be on an equal basis, with a peasant vote counting as much as that of a worker; on a territorial basis, as in the West, rather than according to status (as during Tsarist times) or place of employment; and direct – all Soviets would be elected by the citizens themselves.

> We shall probably adopt our new constitution at
> the end of this year. ... As has been announced
> already, according to the new constitution, the
> suffrage will be universal, equal, direct, and secret.

Most important, Stalin declared that all elections would be contested. Different citizens' organizations would be able to set forth candidates to run against the Communist Party's candidates. Stalin told Howard that citizens would cross off the names of all candidates except those they wished to vote for.

Stalin also stressed the importance of contested elections in fighting bureaucracy.

> You think that there will be no election contests.
> But there will be, and I foresee very lively election
> campaigns. There are not a few institutions in our
> country which work badly. ... Our new electoral
> system will tighten up all institutions and
> organizations and compel them to improve their
> work. Universal, equal, direct and secret suffrage in
> the U.S.S.R. will be a whip in the hands of the
> population against the organs of government which
> work badly. In my opinion our new Soviet
> constitution will be the most democratic
> constitution in the world. (Stalin-Howard 15)

From this point on, Stalin and his closest Politburo associates Viacheslav Molotov and Andrei Zhdanov spoke up for secret, contested elections in all discussions within the Party leadership.

Stalin also insisted that many Soviet citizens who had been deprived of the franchise, called *lishentsy* ("those who have been deprived") should have it restored. These included members of former exploiting classes such as former landlords, and those who had fought against the Bolsheviks during the Civil War of 1918-1921, known as "White Guardists," as well as those convicted of certain crimes (as in the USA today). Most important, and probably most numerous, among the *lishentsy* were two groups: "kulaks," the main targets during the Collectivization movement of a few years before; and those who had violated the 1932 "law of three ears" – who had stolen state property, usually grain (those who stole it to avoid starvation were explicitly exempted from this law).

These electoral reforms would have been unnecessary unless the Stalin leadership wanted to change the manner in which the Soviet Union was governed. They wanted to get the Communist Party out of the business of *directly* running the Soviet Union.

During the Russian Revolution and the critical years that followed, the USSR had been legally governed by an elected hierarchy of soviets (= "councils"), from local to national level, with the Supreme Soviet as the national legislative body, the Council (= *soviet*) of People's Commissars as the executive body, and the Chairman of this Council as the head of state. But in reality, at every level, choice of these officials had always been in the hands of the Bolshevik Party. Elections were held, but direct appointment or nomination by Party leaders (*kooptatsiia*) was also common. Even the elections were controlled by the Party, since no one could run for office unless Party leaders agreed.

To the Bolsheviks, this had made sense. It was the form that the dictatorship of the proletariat took in the specific historical conditions of the revolutionary and post-revolutionary Soviet Union. Under the New Economic Policy, or NEP, the labor and skills of former and current exploiters were needed. But they had to be used only in service to the working class dictatorship – to socialism. They were not to be permitted to rebuild capitalist rela-tionships beyond certain limits, nor to regain political power.

Throughout the 1920s and early 1930s the Bolshevik Party re-cruited aggressively among the working class. By the end of the 1920s most Party members were workers and a high per centage of workers were in the Party. This massive recruitment and huge attempts at political education took place at the same time as the tremendous upheavals of the first Five-Year Plan, crash industri-alization, and the collectivization of individual farms into collective (*kolkhoz*) or soviet farms (*sovkhoz*). The Bolshevik leadership was both sincere in its attempt to "proletarianize" their Party, and suc-cessful in the result.

Stalin and his supporters on the Politburo gave a number of rea-sons for wanting to democratize the Soviet Union. These reasons reflected the Stalin leadership's belief that a new stage of socialism had been reached.

Most peasants were in collective farms. With fewer individual peasant farms every month, the Stalin leadership believed that, objectively, the peasants no longer constituted a separate socio-economic class. Peasants were more like workers than different from them.

Stalin argued that, with the rapid growth of Soviet industry, and especially with the working class holding political power through the Bolshevik Party, the word "proletariat" was no longer accurate. "Proletariat," Stalin averred, referred to the working class under capitalist exploitation, or working under capitalist-type relations of production, such as existed during the first dozen years of the Soviet Union, especially under the NEP. But with direct exploit-ation of workers by capitalists for profit now abolished, the work-ing class should no longer be called the "proletariat."

According to this view, exploiters of labor no longer existed. Workers, now running the country in their own interest through the Bolshevik Party, were no longer like the classic "proletariat." Therefore, the "dictatorship of the proletariat" was no longer an adequate concept. These new conditions called for a new kind of state.

The Anti-Bureaucracy Struggle

The Stalin leadership was also concerned about the Party's role in this new stage of socialism. Stalin himself raised the fight against "bureaucratism" with great vigor as early as his Report to the 17th Party Congress in January 1934. Stalin, Molotov and others called the new electoral system a "weapon against bureaucratization."

Party leaders controlled the government both by determining who entered the Soviets and by exercising various forms of oversight or review over what the government ministries did. Speaking at the 7th Congress of Soviets on February 6, 1935 Molotov said that secret elections "will strike with great force against bureaucratic elements and provide them a useful shock."

Government ministers and their staffs had to know something about the affairs over which they were in charge, if they were to be effective in production. This meant education, usually technical education, in their fields. But Party leaders often made their careers by advancement through Party positions alone. No technical expertise was needed for this kind of advancement. Rather, political criteria were required. These Party officials exercised control, but they themselves often lacked the technical knowledge that could in theory make them skilled at supervision.

This is, apparently, what the Stalin leadership meant by the term "bureaucratism." Though they viewed it as a danger – as, indeed, all Marxists did – they believed it was not inevitable. Rather, they thought that it could be overcome by changing the role of the Party in socialist society. The concept of democracy that Stalin and his supporters in the Party leadership wished to inaugurate in the Soviet Union would necessarily involve a qualitative change in the societal role of the Bolshevik Party.

> Those documents that were accessible to researchers did allow us to understand... that already by the end of the 1930s determined attempts were being undertaken to separate the Party from the state and to limit in a substantive manner the Party's role in the life of the country. (Zhukov, Tainy 8)

Article 3 of the 1936 Constitution reads "In the U.S.S.R. all power belongs to the working people of town and country as represented by the Soviets of Working People's Deputies." The Communist Party is mentioned only in Article 126, as "the vanguard of the working people in their struggle to strengthen and develop the socialist system and is the leading core of all organizations of the working people, both public and state." That is, the Party was to lead *organizations* but not the legislative or executive organs of the state.

Once the Party was out of direct control over society, Stalin believed, its role should be confined to agitation and propaganda, and participation in the selection of cadres. What would this have meant? Perhaps something like this:

* The Party would revert to its essential function of winning people to the ideals of communism as they understood it.

* This would mean the end of cushy sinecure-type jobs, and a reversion to the style of hard work and selfless dedication that characterized the Bolsheviks during the Tsarist period, the Revolution and Civil War, the period of NEP, and the very hard period of crash industrialization and collectivization.

During these periods Party membership, for most, meant hard work and sacrifice, often among non-Party members, many of whom were hostile to the Bolsheviks. It meant the need for a real base among the masses.

Stalin insisted that Communists should be hard-working, educated people, able to make a real contribution to production and to the creation of a communist society. Stalin himself was an indefatigable student.

To summarize, the evidence suggests that Stalin intended the new electoral system to accomplish the following goals:

* Make sure that only technically trained people led, in production and in Soviet society at large;

* Stop the degeneration of the Bolshevik Party, and return Party members, especially leaders, to their primary function: giving po-

litical and moral leadership, by example and persuasion, to the rest of society;

* Strengthen the Party's mass work;

* Win the support of the country's citizens behind the government;

* Create the basis for a classless, communist society.

Stalin's Defeat

During 1935, under the aegis of Andrei Vyshinskii, Chief Prosecutor of the USSR, many citizens who had been exiled, imprisoned, and – most significantly for our present purposes – deprived of the franchise, were restored. Hundreds of thousands of former kulaks, richer farmers who were the main target of collectivization, and of those who had been imprisoned or exiled for resisting collectivization in some way, were freed. The enfranchised population was expanded by at least hundreds of thousands of people who had reason to feel that State and Party had treated them unfairly.

At the June 1937 Central Committee Plenum Iakov A. Iakovlev, one of those who had worked on the draft of the new constitution, said that the suggestion for contested elections was made by Stalin himself. This suggestion seems to have met with widespread, albeit tacit, opposition from the regional Party leaders, the First Secretaries. After the Howard interview there was not even the nominal praise or support for Stalin's statement about contested elections in the central newspapers – those most under the direct control of the Politburo. *Pravda* carried one article only, on March 10, and it did not mention contested elections.

From this historian Iurii N. Zhukov concludes:

> This could mean only one thing. Not only the 'broad
> leadership' [the regional First Secretaries], but at
> least a part of the Central Committee apparatus,
> Agitprop under Stetskii and Tal', did not accept
> Stalin's innovation, did not want to approve, even in
> a purely formal manner, contested elections,
> dangerous to many, which, as followed from those
> of Stalin's words that *Pravda* did underscore,
> directly threatened the positions and real power of

> the First Secretaries – the Central Committees of
> the national communist parties, the regional,
> oblast', city, and area committees. (Zhukov, Inoi
> 211)

The Party First Secretaries held Party offices from which they
could not be removed by defeat in any elections to the Soviets they
might enter. But the immense local power they held stemmed from
the Party's control over every aspect of the economy and state
apparatus – kolkhoz, factory, education, military. The new electoral system would deprive the First Secretaries of their automatic
positions as delegates to the Soviets, and of their ability to simply
choose the other delegates. Defeat of themselves or of "their" candidates (the Party candidates) in elections to the soviets would be,
in effect, a referendum on their work.

A First Secretary whose candidates were defeated at the polls by
non-Party candidates would be exposed as someone with weak
ties to the masses. During the campaigns, opposition candidates
were sure to make campaign issues out of any corruption, authori-
tarianism, or incompetence they observed among Party officials.
Defeated candidates would be shown up to have serious weak-
nesses as communists, and this would probably lead to their being
replaced.

Senior Party leaders were usually Party members of many years'
standing, veterans of the really dangerous days of Tsarist times,
the Revolution, the Civil War, and collectivization, when to be a
communist was fraught with peril and difficulty. Many had little
formal education. Unlike Stalin or Beria, it seems that most of them
were unwilling or unable to "remake themselves" through self-
education.

All of these men were long-time supporters of Stalin's policies.
They had implemented the collectivization of the peasantry – a
step essential to escape the cycle of famines — during which hundreds of thousands had been deported. During 1932-33 perhaps as
many as three million, had died by a famine that had not been
"man-made," despite anticommunist claims to the contrary. These
Party leaders had been in charge of crash industrialization, again

under necessarily severe conditions of poor housing, insufficient food and medical care, low pay and few goods to buy with it.

Now they faced elections in which those formerly deprived of the franchise because they had been in opposition to these Soviet policies would suddenly have the right to vote restored. It's likely that they feared many would vote against their candidates, or against *any* Bolshevik candidate.

Trials, Conspiracies, Repression

Plans for the new constitution and elections had been outlined during the June 1936 Plenum of the Central Committee. The delegates unanimously approved the draft Constitution. But none of them spoke up in favor of it. This failure to give at least lip service to a Stalin proposal certainly indicated latent opposition.

During the 8th All-Russian Congress of Soviets meeting in November-December 1936 Stalin and Molotov again stressed the value of widening the franchise and of secret and contested elections. In the spirit of Stalin's interview with Howard, Molotov again stressed the beneficial effect, for the Party, of permitting non-communist candidates for the Soviets:

> This system ... cannot but strike against those who have become bureaucratized, alienated from the masses. ... will facilitate the promotion of new forces... that must come forth to replace backward or bureaucratized [*ochinovnivshimsya*] elements. Under the new form of elections the election of enemy elements is possible. But even this danger, in the last analysis, must serve to help us, insofar as it will serve as a lash to those organizations that need it, and to [Party] workers who have fallen asleep. (Zhukov, Repressii 15).

Stalin himself put it even more strongly:

> ... if the people here and there elected hostile forces, this will mean that our agitational work is poorly organized, and that we have fully deserved this disgrace. (Zhukov, Inoi 293; Stalin, "Draft").

This was Stalin's position, and once again the First Secretaries showed tacit hostility to it. We do not really know why. Did they consider Stalin's proposal to be a violation of the dictatorship of the proletariat? Did they regard it as too great a concession to capitalist concepts of democracy? Even in the most "democratic" of capitalist states, avowed enemies of capitalism are not permitted to participate freely in elections unless pro-capitalist parties have overwhelming advantages. And even in those states, the system – capitalism or socialism – is never "up for grabs."

The December 1936 Central Committee Plenum, whose session overlapped with the Congress, met on December 4th. But there was virtually no discussion of the first agenda item, the draft Constitution. Ezhov's report, "On Trotskyite and Right Anti-Soviet Organizations," was far more central to the C.C. members' concerns.

On December 5 1936 the Congress approved the draft of the new Constitution. But there had been little real discussion. Instead, the delegates – Party leaders – had emphasized the threats from enemies foreign and domestic. Rather than giving speeches of approval for the Constitution, which was the main topic reported on by Stalin, Molotov, Zhdanov, Maksim Litvinov, and Vyshinskii, the delegates virtually ignored it. A Commission was set up for further study of the draft Constitution, with nothing fixed about contested elections

The international situation was indeed tense. Victory for fascism in the Spanish Civil War was only a question of time. The Soviet Union was surrounded by hostile powers. By the second half of the 1930s, *all* of these countries were headed by fiercely authoritarian, militaristic, anti-communist and anti-Soviet regimes. In October 1936 Finland had fired across the Soviet frontier. That same month the "Berlin-Rome Axis" was formed by Hitler and Mussolini. A month later, Japan joined Nazi Germany and fascist Italy to form the "Anti-Comintern Pact." Soviet efforts at military alliances against Nazi Germany met with rejection in the capitals of the West.

While the Congress was attending to the new Constitution the Soviet leadership was between the first two large-scale Moscow Trials. Zinoviev and Kamenev had gone on trial along with some others in August 1936. The second trial, in January 1937, involved some of the major followers of Trotsky, led by Iurii Piatakov, until recently the deputy Commissar of Heavy Industry.

Chapter 2. Conspiracy

In 1898, the Russian Social Democratic Labour Party was formed as the Marxist party of the Russian Empire. In 1903 it experienced a major split into Bolshevik ("majority") and Menshevik ("minority") factions. The Bolshevik faction was led by Vladimir Lenin (Vladimir Il'ich Ul'ianov). This split became more marked when the majority of the Mensheviks supported Russia in the World War. In 1918 the Bolsheviks changed their name to the All-Russian Communist Party (bolshevik) to distinguish themselves from the Socialist International or Social-Democrats.

Factional disputes, which had existed in the Bolshevik Party before 1918, intensified after the Revolution of November 1917 and during the ensuing Civil War. Some of them, like the bitter dispute over whether or not to sign a separate peace with Germany, were reflected in the later factional splits of the 1920s.

When the Civil War was over the Bolshevik Party was faced with rebuilding a largely shattered society and constructing socialism. All had hoped that socialist revolutions in some of the advanced capitalist countries of Western Europe would help backward Russia. But the attempts at such revolutions in Hungary and Germany were crushed.

The Bolsheviks were left to figure out how to build socialism by themselves. There was no blueprint, no guidelines aside from some very general remarks by Marx and Engels who, after all, also lacked any relevant experience. Disagreements over Party policy took place at the Party Congresses, held once a year from 1917 (the VI Congress) until 1925 (the XIV Congress).

Factions were formed along the lines of the principal disagreements. Factional organizing also continued outside the meetings of the Party Congresses. The principle of democratic centralism was understood to mean that all Party members were required to support the political decisions taken by the Party Congresses. The continuation of factions outside the Congresses was in contradiction to this principle.

At the X Party Congress in 1921 a resolution banning party factions was passed by a large margin. Nevertheless, factions continued to exist. But factions had been banned, and since all Party members were obliged to carry out the decisions of the Party Congresses, most factional activity now took place in a clandestine manner.

The factions formed around certain well-known party figures. In 1926 and 1927 the Zinoviev and Trotsky factions joined forces to form the United Opposition. In 1927 a number of its members were expelled from the Party for factionalizing. Most of them soon rejoined, after pledging to follow the Party's line. But it was clear that they had not abandoned their dissenting view. In fact the Party majority, led by Stalin, did not demand that they do so.

At the 10th Anniversary of the Revolution in November 1927 the United Opposition attempted to lead a counter-demonstration. It was broken up by the police. Soon after this Leon Trotsky, who refused to reconcile to the Party majority, was exiled to Alma-Ata.[1] There Trotsky continued his factional activity and in January 1929 he was exiled from the Soviet Union and moved to Istanbul, Turkey.

The Bloc of Oppositionists

At the public Moscow trials of 1936, 1937, and 1938 the prosecution charged that a clandestine and, from the Party's standpoint, illegal bloc of the various opposition groups was formed in 1932 and continued to conspire against the Stalin leadership. During Khrushchev's time, and again during the period of Mikhail Gorbachev's leadership of the Soviet Party and state, these conspiracies were declared to have been inventions, fabrications by Stalin and his men for the purpose of justifying the repression and murder of their supposed members.

---

[1] Today named Almaty, the largest city in Kazakhstan.

From exile in France, then Norway, and finally in Mexico, Leon Trotsky vigorously denied that he and his followers had joined or ever would join such a bloc. But in 1980 Pierre Broué, at that time the most prominent Trotskyist historian in the world, discovered evidence in the Harvard Trotsky Archive that this bloc did in fact exist and that Trotsky had approved it.[2]

During the next dozen years Broué continued to work in the Harvard Trotsky Archive and in another archive of Trotsky's writings preserved at the Hoover Institution in Stanford, California. He discovered more evidence that Trotsky had falsely denied some of the charges against him made at the Moscow Trials. American researcher Arch Getty discovered that Trotsky had indeed remained in contact with prominent supporters in the USSR like Karl Radek and Ivan Smirnov who had publicly renounced their Trotskyist views and with whom Trotsky claimed to have broken off contact.

Since the end of the Soviet Union in 1991 a great many documents from former Soviet archives have been published in Russia. Research based on these documents, together with other materials, has transformed our understanding of Soviet history during the Stalin period. One important discovery is that Nikita Khrushchev's accusations against Stalin in his famous "Secret Speech" to the XX Party Congress in February, 1956 are all false (Furr, Khrushchev).

On December 1, 1934 Sergei M. Kirov, First Secretary of the Leningrad oblast' and city Party Committees, was murdered in Party headquarters at the Smolny Institute in Leningrad. The Stalin-led Soviet government stated that their investigation proved that the assassin, Leonid Vasil'evich Nikolaev, had acted on behalf of a secret Zinovievist group.

Trotsky claimed that this could not be true and that Stalin was falsifying whatever had really happened. We know now that Trotsky himself had something to do with Kirov's murder. Khrushchev's and, later, Gorbachev's men claimed that no secret Zinovievist group existed and that Nikolaev had been a lone assassin. Western

---

[2] For a fuller discussion of Broue's discoveries and Trotsky's lies in general see Furr, Amalgams.

anticommunist scholars either echoed Khrushchev and Gorbachev or claimed that Stalin had had Kirov killed. Thanks to evidence from the former Soviet archives and the Trotsky archives we now know that the Stalin-era police and prosecution were correct.[3]

Further evidence was uncovered by the Soviet police in 1936. At the first Moscow Trial of August 1936, often called the Zinoviev-Kamenev trial, both Zinoviev and Kamenev confessed to collaborating in Kirov's murder. They admitted that a bloc of oppositionists including Zinovievists, Trotskyists, and others did exist whose goal was to seize power in the USSR by violence. Other Trotskyists confessed to plotting assassinations of Soviet leaders, Stalin included.

The former Soviet archives have disclosed some pretrial interrogations and confessions of these defendants. We also have the texts of the appeals of their death sentences by most of these defendants to the Soviet Supreme Court. In them they repeat their guilt in unequivocal terms.

The defendants in the 1936 Moscow Trial had disclosed the existence of a parallel leadership for the bloc and had named Trotskyists and Rightists as participants. Trotskyists named included Karl Radek and Iurii Piatakov. Rightist leaders named included Mikhail Tomsky, Aleksei Rykov, and Nikolai Bukharin.

Among those convinced by the evidence was Sergo Ordzhonikidze, Commissar for Heavy Industry and Piatakov's superior. Documents from former Soviet archives make it clear that the story, first recorded by Khrushchev and his men, that Ordzhonikidze had opposed Piatakov's prosecution, is false. Khrushchev also claimed that Ordzhonikidze had committed suicide in despair over Stalin's wrongful persecution of Piatakov and others. This tale too has been proven false.[4]

Between September and December 1936 Radek, Piatakov, and others involved with them revealed details about Trotsky's con-

---

[3] For a full discussion of the evidence, and discussion of the coverup by Khrushchev, Gorbachev, and all mainstream historians to this day see Furr, Kirov.

[4] See Bobrov, Taina.

spiracies with Hitler's Germany and with anti-Soviet and pro-
fascist forces inside the USSR. At the second Moscow Trial in January 1937 the defendants detailed Trotsky's plans to dismantle
socialism in the USSR in exchange for German and Japanese support in seizing power in the USSR. They implicated Bukharin,
Rykov, and other Rightists as members of the bloc, fully informed
about Trotsky's plans.

During December 1936 and January 1937 Bukharin had face-to-
face confrontations with some of his accusers: E.F. Kulikov and
Iurii Piatakov on December 7, 1936; Karl Radek and Valentin
Astrov on January 13, 1937. All these men accused Bukharin of
being in a clandestine opposition that aimed to assassinate Stalin.[5]

In the case of Valentin Astrov, we can be confident that he was telling the truth. In 1989 and again in 1993 Astrov, by now very aged,
had the opportunity to retract his accusations against Bukharin.
But he retracted only his claim that he had heard Bukharin use the
word "terror." He also affirmed that the NKVD had treated him
politely, never even raising their voices. If Astrov had wanted to
claim that he had been tortured he could have easily done so. But
he insisted that this had not happened.

Until February 1937 the NKVD continued to send to Bukharin confessions by other Rightists, some of them Bukharin's former students, accusing Bukharin of being a leader of the secret bloc of
Trotskyists, Rightists and others. Bukharin said that the investigators sent him as many as 20 such confessions against him in a single day. This enormous amount of evidence virtually guaranteed
that Bukharin would face arrest and trial.

On February 5 Ordzhonikidze gave a talk to managers of the
Commissariat of Heavy Industry in which he made it clear that he
firmly believed that Piatakov had betrayed them all and had used
his position as Ordzhonikidze's assistant to do enormous harm to
the industrialization of the Soviet Union. (Getty & Naumov 292-4).

---

[5] See Bukharin-Kulikov; Bukharin-Piatakov; Bukharin-Astrov. For Astrov's statements in
1989 and 1993 see Furr, Kirov 318-319.

On February 18 Ordzhonikidze died. In the evening of February 23 the Central Committee Plenum convened. It was to be by far the longest and most dramatic CC meeting in the history of the Bolshevik Party.

Chapter 3. Convergence of Conspiracy and Elections

The February-March Plenum of the Central Committee, the longest ever held in the history of the USSR, dragged on for two weeks. Almost nothing was known about it until 1992, when the plenum's huge transcript began to be published in *Voprosy Istorii* – a process that took the journal almost four years to complete.

This plenum dramatized the contradictory tasks that confronted the Party leadership: the struggle against internal enemies, and the need to prepare for secret, contested elections under the new Constitution by year's end. The gradual discovery of more and more groups conspiring to overthrow the Soviet government demanded police action. But to prepare for truly democratic elections to the government, and to improve inner-party democracy – a theme stressed over and over by those closest to Stalin in the Politburo – required the opposite: openness to criticism and self-criticism, secret elections of leaders by rank-and-file Party members, and an end to "cooptation" by First Secretaries.

> Alongside the discussion of former oppositionists, party leaders introduced two new concepts: democracy (demokratiia) and criticism of authority. ... Stalin, Zhdanov, and N. M. Shvernik, the head of the All-Union Central Council of Trade Unions, emphasized the need for multicandidate, secret-ballot elections for posts within the Party, the soviets, and the unions. Contending that the political culture had become increasingly ossified, self-serving, and bureaucratic, they invited the rank and file to reinvigorate their governing institutions. ... The plenum strongly urged not only rank-and-file party and union members but also ordinary citizens to challenge their local and regional leaders and

rebuild democracy from below. (Goldman,
Inventing 65)

Party leaders, insisting on democracy and
multicandidate, secret-ballot elections, attempted
to bust up the controlling "family circles" within the
unions and party organizations. They urged the
rank and file to exercise their democratic rights,
expose hidden oppositionists, and oust entrenched
leaders from power. (Goldman, Terror 96)

The plenum... was a rich and complicated affair.
The "new wave of mass repression" was prompted
not only by the arrest of Bukharin and Rykov, but,
more importantly, also by a new and
unprecedented emphasis on "democracy." Several
keynote speakers, including Stalin and A. A.
Zhdanov, secretary of the Central Committee and
the Leningrad regional and city committees,
stressed the need for multicandidate, secret ballot
elections for posts within the Party, the soviets, and
the unions. They sharply criticized a political
culture that had grown increasingly ossified and
bureaucratic, stressing the need to reinvigorate
governing institutions from below.... Party leaders,
angry at the inability of lower organizations to
purge themselves of oppositionists, moved to
mobilize the rank and file. Democracy was thus a
way to increase support, invigorate the rank and
file. (Goldman, Terror 110-111)

Ezhov's report about the continuing investigations into conspiracies within the country was overshadowed by Nikolai Bukharin,
who, in loquacious attempts to confess past misdeeds, distance
himself from onetime associates, and assure everyone of his current loyalty, managed only to incriminate himself further. (Thurston, 40-42; Getty & Naumov 563)

After three whole days of this Zhdanov spoke about the need for greater democracy both in the country and in the Party, invoking the struggle against bureaucracy and the need for closer ties to the masses, both party and non-party.

> The new electoral system … will give a powerful push towards the improvement of the work of Soviet bodies, the liquidation of bureaucratic bodies, the liquidation of bureaucratic shortcomings, and deformations in the work of our Soviet organizations. And these shortcomings, as you know, are very substantial. Our Party bodies must be ready for the electoral struggle. In the elections we will have to deal with hostile agitation and hostile candidates. (Zhukov, Inoi 343)

Zhdanov spoke out strongly for democracy in the Party as well.

> This meant secret ballot re-election of all party organs from top to bottom, periodic reporting of party organs to their organizations, strict party discipline, and subordination of the minority to the majority, and unconditional obligatory decisions of higher bodies on all party members. He complained about co-option (appointment) to party buros rather than election, and candidates for leading positions being considered behind closed doors, 'in family order'. When he called this 'familyness [*semeistvennost'*]' Stalin interjected, 'it is a deal' [*sgovor*, literally, a marriage agreement]. This was a virtual declaration of war against the regional clan leaderships, and their reaction in the discussion to Zhdanov's report (which they at first unprecedentedly greeted with angry silence) showed that they were angry. (Getty, Rise 77)[1]

Goldman agrees:

---

[1] Zhdanov's presentation was on the evening of February 26, 1937. It is in *Voprosy Istorii* 5 (1993) 3-14.

In his keynote speech on the erosion of democracy within the Party, Zhdanov advanced the idea that the Party needed to empower the rank and file. He highlighted the widespread practice of *kooptatsiia* or "appointments," which had replaced elections in staffing posts. *Kooptatsiia* promoted the formation of tight cliques, loyal only to the leader who appointed them. The practice had become so common that some local organizations did not have a single elected official....Moreover, when elections were held, the results were predetermined. Several days before a party conference, Zhdanov explained, the secretary of the primary party organization would "go into a corner somewhere" and draw up a list of candidates. The list would be formalized in advance in a small closed meeting, and the election "transformed into a simple formality" lasting no more than twenty minutes. Zhdanov complained that this "back-door" decision-making was "a violation of the legal rights of party members and of party democracy."

- (Goldman, Terror 118.)

Nikolai Shvernik, representing the Stalin leadership of the Party, also issued a strong call for democracy in the trade unions.

Shvernik argued that the unions, like the Party, lacked internal democracy.

"1 should say here, directly and with all frankness," he explained, "that the unions are in even worse shape." With the development of new industries during the first five-year plan, the country's 47 unions had split into 165, creating thousands of new jobs. Positions at every level were filled by appointment, rather than election....Shvernik concluded his speech with the suggestion that elections were needed not only in the Party, but in the unions as well. (Goldman, Terror 126)

The 6th Plenum of the All-Union Central Council [Soviet] of Professional Unions (VTsSPS), the Soviet trade union federation, met
from April 24 to May 15, 1937, after the February-March CC Plenum.[2] Goldman states:

> New elections based on secret ballots were to be
> held in every union organization from central to
> factory committees. Union members would have
> "the unlimited right to reject and criticize"
> individual candidates. Voting by lists was
> forbidden. (Goldman, Terror 141)

Speaking for the Stalin leadership Zhdanov foresaw electoral con-
tests with non-party candidates that seriously opposed developments in the Soviet Union. This fact alone is utterly incompatible
with Cold-War and Khrushchevite accounts. Zhdanov also emphasized, at length, the need to develop democratic norms within
the Bolshevik Party itself.

> If we want to win the respect of our Soviet and
> Party workers to our laws, and the masses – to the
> Soviet constitution, then we must guarantee the
> restructuring [perestroika] of Party work on the
> basis of an indubitable and full implementation of
> the bases of inner-party democracy, which is
> outlined in the bylaws of our Party.

He enumerated the essential measures, already contained in the
draft resolution to his report: the elimination of appointment; a
ban on voting by slates; a guarantee "of the unlimited right for
members of the Party to set aside the nominated candidates and of
the unlimited right to criticize these candidates." (Zhukov, Inoi
345)

Party Secretaries' Fear of Elections

Zhdanov's report was drowned by discussion of other agenda
items, mainly discussions about "enemies." A number of First

---

[2] "Obshchenatsional'nye s"ezdy profsoiuzov Rossii i SSSR, plenumy VTsSPS." At
http://istprof.ru/2062.html

Secretaries responded with alarm that those who were, or might be expected to be, preparing most assiduously for the Soviet elections were *opponents* of Soviet power: Social-Revolutionaries, the priesthood, and other "enemies."[3]

> As early as October 1936, deputy NKVD chief G. A. Molchanov had written to Politburo members about how kulaks and anti-Soviet elements were disrupting election meetings. He wrote about how kulak elements were spreading provocative rumours 'in connection with the publication of the new constitution' about the dissolution of the collective farms and reopening of churches. He quoted one kolkhoznik, 'Soon we will get an order that we can leave the kolkhozes. It's the end of the communists.' In January 1937, a special NKVD report quoted several peasants, including one who said, 'The new constitution gives us special settlers rights as citizens of the USSR. In a few days, everyone will go home. The first thing we will do is settle scores with those activists who dekulakized and deported us, and then we'll go somewhere where they can't find us.' (Getty, Fever 228)

Apprehension about the outcome of elections to the Soviets was shared even by the Stalin leadership.

> Although the plenum delegates uniformly praised the new constitution, they were deeply concerned about the outcome of the upcoming elections. Many feared that the Party lacked sufficient support to maintain its predominant political position. Zhdanov noted gravely that the introduction of democratic elections was "a very serious exam [test

---

[3] Getty notes that CC members pointedly refused to respond to Zhdanov's speech, putting the Chair, Andreev, into confusion (Excesses 124). Zhukov places less emphasis on this, as Eikhe and other First Secretaries did reply at the next session, while emphasizing the struggle against "enemies." (Inoi 345)

> – GF] for our Party." A gallows humor, based on
> anxiety that the Party might not weather a genuine
> referendum on its leadership, characterized many
> of the delegates' comments. ... Zhdanov warned that
> the Party, lacking experience with secret-ballot
> elections and individual candidates, would face
> "enemy agitation and enemy candidates." Religious
> groups were already reviving and petitioning to
> reopen the churches. (Goldman, Terror 116)

Molotov replied with a report stressing, once again, "the development and strengthening of self-criticism," and directly opposed the
search for "enemies":

> There's no point in searching for people to blame,
> comrades. If you prefer, all of us here are to blame,
> beginning with the Party's central institutions and
> ending with the lowest Party organizations.
> (Zhukov, Inoi 349)

But those who followed Molotov to the podium ignored his report
and continued to harp on the necessity of "searching out 'enemies',
of exposing 'wreckers', and the struggle against 'wrecking'." (352)
When he spoke again Molotov marvelled that there had been almost no attention paid to the substance of his report, which he repeated, after first summarizing what *was* being done against internal enemies.

Stalin's speech of March 3 was likewise divided, returning at the
end to the need for improving Party work and of weeding out incapable Party members and replacing them with new ones. Like
Molotov's, Stalin's report was virtually ignored.

From the beginning of the discussions Stalin's fears were under-
standable. It seemed he had run into a deaf wall of incomprehension, of the unwillingness of the CC members, who heard in the
report just what they wanted to hear, to discuss what he wanted
them to discuss. Of the 24 persons who took part in the discussions, 15 spoke mainly about "enemies of the people," that is, Trotskyists. They spoke with conviction, aggressively, just as they had
after the reports by Zhdanov and Molotov. They reduced all the

problems to one – the necessity of searching out "enemies." And practically none of them recalled Stalin's main point – about the shortcomings in the work of Party organizations, about preparation for the elections to the Supreme Soviet. (Zhukov, Inoi 357)

The Stalin leadership stepped up the attack on the First Secretaries. Iakovlev criticized Moscow Party leader Khrushchev, among others, for unjustified expulsions of Party members. Malenkov seconded his criticism of Party secretaries for their indifference to rank-and-file members. This seems to have stimulated the CC members to stop speaking temporarily about enemies, but only in order to begin defending themselves. There was still no response to Stalin's report. (Zhukov, Inoi 358-60)

In his final speech on March 5, the concluding day of the Plenum, Stalin minimized the need to hunt enemies, even Trotskyists, many of whom, he said, had turned towards the Party. His main theme was the need to remove Party officials from running every aspect of the economy, to fight bureaucracy, and to raise the political level of Party officials.

Stalin had upped the ante in the criticism of the First Secretaries:

> Some comrades among us think that, if they are a
> People's Commissar, then they know everything.
> They believe that rank, in and of itself, grants very
> great, almost inexhaustible knowledge. Or they
> think: If I am a Central Committee member, then I
> am not one by accident, then I must know
> everything. This is not the case. (Stalin,
> Zakliuchitel'noe; Zhukov, Inoi 360-1)

Most ominously for all Party officials, including First Secretaries, Stalin stated that each of them should choose two cadre to take their places while they attended six-month political education courses that would soon be established. With replacement officials in their stead, Party secretaries might well have feared that they could easily be reassigned during this period, breaking the back of their "families" (officials subservient to them), a major feature of bureaucracy. (Zhukov, Inoi 362)

Thurston characterizes Stalin's speech as "considerably milder," stressing "the need to learn from the masses and pay attention to criticism from below." Even the resolution passed on the basis of Stalin's report touches on "enemies" only briefly, and dealt mainly with failings in party organizations and their leaderships. According to Zhukov, who quotes from this unpublished resolution, not a single one of its 25 points was mainly concerned with "enemies." (Thurston, Life 48-9; Zhukov, Inoi 362-4)

Stalin's speech too touches only very briefly on the subject of "enemies" and even then to warn the CC against "beating" everyone who had once been a Trotskyist. Stalin insists that there are "remarkable people" among former Trotskyists, specifically naming Feliks Dzerzhinsky.

Chapter 4. From the February-March 1937 CC Plenum to the June 1937 CC Plenum

After the February-March 1937 Plenum the First Secretaries staged a virtual rebellion. First Stalin, and then the Politburo, sent out messages re-emphasizing the need to conduct secret Party elections, opposition to appointment rather than election, and the need for inner-Party democracy generally. The First Secretaries were doing things in the old way, regardless of the resolutions of the Plenum.

During the next few months Stalin and his closest associates tried to turn the focus away from a hunt for internal enemies – the largest concern of the CC members – and back towards fighting bureaucracy in the Party and preparing for the Soviet elections. Meanwhile, "local party leaders did everything they could within the limits of party discipline (and sometimes outside it) to stall or change the elections." (Getty, Excesses 126; Zhukov, Inoi 367-71)

But a very ominous period loomed. In late March 1937 Genrikh Iagoda, head of the NKVD, was arrested. In April he began to confess to having played an important role in the secret bloc of oppositionists that had been the main target of the First and Second Moscow Trials.

During the January 1937 Moscow Trial Karl Radek had warned against the danger of Trotskyist elements in Spain. Soviet intelligence had information that German and Francoist agents were active in stirring up the revolt as well. At the beginning of May 1937 an armed revolt erupted in Spain against the Spanish Republican government. Among the leading figures in the revolt were Andres Nin, a former political aide to Trotsky, Erwin Wolf, Trotsky's emissary in Spain, and Kurt Landau, a militant opponent of the Stalin leadership who had been an active Trotskyist and was still politically close to him. The POUM party, of which Nin was a leader, had consistently taken pro-Trotsky and anti-Stalin positions.

More shocking discoveries were to come. In May and early June 1937 high-ranking military commanders confessed to conspiring with the German General Staff to defeat the Red Army in the case of an invasion of the USSR by Germany and its allies, and also to being linked to conspiracies by political figures, including many who still occupied high positions. (Getty, Excesses 115, 135; Thurston, Rise 70, 90,101-2) Other prominent Party leaders were arrested in connection with the military conspiracy, including Ian Rudzutak, a candidate member of the Politburo.

This situation was far more serious than anything the Soviet government, or any modern government, had faced before. In the case of the 1936 and 1937 Moscow Trials the government had taken some time to prepare the case and organize a public trial for maximum publicity. But the military conspiracy was handled far differently. A little more than three weeks passed from the date of Marshal Mikhail Tukhachevsky's arrest in late May to the trial and execution of Tukhachevsky and seven other high-ranking military commanders on June 11-12. Dozens of high-ranking military commanders were recalled to Moscow to read the evidence against their colleagues – for most of them, their superiors – and to listen to alarmed analyses by Stalin and Marshal Voroshilov, People's Commissar for Defence and the highest ranking military figure in the country.

The Politburo had planned that the Constitutional reforms be the central agenda item at the upcoming June 1937 Plenum. But by June the situation was different. The discovery of plots by the former chief of the NKVD and by top military leaders to overthrow the government and kill its leading members entirely changed the political atmosphere.

In his June 2 speech to the expanded session of the Military Soviet Stalin portrayed the series of recently uncovered conspiracies as limited and largely successfully dealt with. At the February-March Plenum he and his Politburo supporters had minimized the First Secretaries' overriding concern with internal enemies. But the situation was "slowly, but decisively, getting out of his [Stalin's] control." (Stalin, Vystuplenie; Zhukov, Inoi Ch. 16, *passim*; 411).

Iagoda and the military commanders around Tukhachevsky named many other high-ranking Party members who were involved in the network of conspiracies, including Central Committee members and candidate members. Among them was Avel' Enukidze. In 1935 Enukidze had been removed from his post in the Kremlin and expelled from the Party for negligence in permitting conspirators to find employment in the Kremlin but he had been readmitted to the Party in June 1936. Now he was rearrested. In April 1937 began to confess to his part in the conspiracy to carry out an armed *coup d'état.*

Bukharin, along with Aleksei Rykov, had been arrested during the February-March 1937 CC Plenum. For three months he continued to maintain his innocence. Abruptly on June 2, 1937 Bukharin reversed his position and made a lengthy confession of guilt. Some have speculated that Bukharin may have been prompted to do so upon hearing of the arrest of Tukhachevsky and the other commanders. Perhaps he had been hoping that he would be released after a successful military *coup* against Stalin.

Between the end of the February-March 1937 CC Plenum on March 5, 1937, and the opening of the June CC Plenum on June 23, 1937, 18 members of the Central Committee and 20 candidate members were arrested for participation in the anti-Soviet conspiracy. Their expulsions were voted on at the June Plenum.

The Conspiracies Were Genuine

In his source book (with Oleg V. Naumov) on the Bolshevik Party during the 1930s Arch Getty writes:

> It is, of course, difficult to know the inner thoughts
> of the top leaders about the degree of guilt of those
> they destroyed. But if the following rare example of
> their private correspondence is typical, there
> apparently was little difference between the
> Stalinist leaders' private thoughts and their public

positions. They seem really to have believed[1] in the existence of a far-flung conspiracy. (Getty & Naumov 455)

On June 19, 1937 Stalin received a telegram, addressed to the Soviet government, sent by Trotsky from his exile in Mexico. In it Trotsky stated that Stalin's policies would lead "to external and internal collapse." On it Stalin signed his name and wrote: "Dirty spy! Brazen spy of Hitler!" It was also signed by Molotov, Voroshilov, Mikoian, and Zhdanov. Clearly they all believed that Trotsky really was in contact with the Germans. Given Tukhachevsky's confession and Marshal Budennyi' comments on the Tukhachevsky trial, there can no doubt that this conspiracy did exist.

The collection cited above of Iagoda's interrogation-confessions and other materials consists mainly of investigators' interrogations of Iagoda and a few of his associates and Iagoda's confessions of involvement in the conspiracy to carry out a coup against the Soviet government; Trotsky's leadership of the conspiracy; and, in general, all that Iagoda confessed to in the 1938 Trial. There is no indication that these confessions were other than genuine. The volume's editors deny that any of the facts cited in the interrogations are accurate, and declare the interrogations themselves "falsified." But they do not give any evidence that this is the case.

Jansen and Petrov (p. 226 n. 9) though very anti-Stalin, cite this volume as evidence and without comment. Furthermore, there is good evidence that this was so in fact – that these conspiracies did exist, that the confessions given at the public trials were genuine rather than coerced, and that the major charges against the defendants were true. Other large volumes of primary documents contain a great many NKVD reports of conspiracies and texts of interrogations. We will discuss them in the following chapters.

The most plausible explanation for the existence of all this evidence is that much of it, and perhaps all of it, is true. We also have

---

[1] Getty and Naumov do not believe that such conspiracies existed.

a great deal of evidence concerning the Tukhachevsky Affair. All of it points to the guilt of the military men.[2]

---

[2] For detailed, evidenced discussions of the Tukhachevsky Affair see Furr, Kirov Chapter 17, and Furr, Amalgams Chapters 10-12.

Chapter 5. The June 1937 Central Committee Plenum

On June 17, 1937, just prior to the June CC plenum, Nikolai Ezhov, who had replaced Iagoda as head (commissar) of the NKVD, transmitted a message from S.N. Mironov, NKVD chief in Western Siberia, reporting the threat of revolts by subversives in concert with Japanese intelligence. In it Mironov reported that Robert I. Eikhe, Party First Secretary of Western Siberia, would request the ability to form a "troika" to deal with this threat.

We also have one of the reports Mironov sent to Ezhov and clearly intended to be forwarded to Stalin to justify this request. These were to be crucial in the inception of the mass repressions that followed the Plenum.

> June 22, 1937
>
> No 58010
>
> Top secret
>
> To Comrade Stalin
>
>
> I hereby direct to you a brief report by the chief of the UNKVD of the Western Siberian krai com. [S.N.] Mironov. I consider that it is essential to allow the formation in this krai of a *troika* for the purposes of extra-judicial review of cases concerning the liquidated anti-Soviet insurgent organizations.
>
> People's Commissar for Internal Affairs
>
> Commissar of State Security Ezhov

I direct to you a report on the combined cases of the 3 and 4 sections of the UGB [Directorate of State Security] concerning the S-R and ROVS underground.

The 3rd section has been conducting the investigation concerning the liquidated agent case "Aristocratia" of the Cadet-monarchist organization ROVS, which includes a group of exiled princes, noblemen, and former officers, and has crushed the groups of S-Rs and insurgents.

The 4th section has developed the case of the Siberian Bureau of the S-Rs, after the discovery of the fighting S-R organization headed by General Eskin and has crushed the ROVS insurgent movement....

On this matter, considering that the development of the case ...will probably exceed considerably the number of participants that we have already uncovered, your special authorization is needed.

[...]

2) It is desirable, on the one hand, to accelerate the sending to me of a visiting session of the Military Tribunal [of the Supreme Court] to consider the cases of Japanese-German, Trotskyist, espionage, and other cases in the order previously stipulated. The cases against 500 persons will be formulated in the coming days. And, on the other hand, **either to give us the right on the spot, in a simplified procedure**, through a special college of the krai court or a special *troika*, to carry out capital punishment in the S-R / ROVS cases, which is where most of the kulaks are concentrated, or the exiled former White officers ...

Com. Eikhe, to whom I have given one copy of this report, is preparing to request the agreement to

create *troikas* from the proper authorities.
(Khaustov & Samuel'son pp.332-3.)

Robert Eikhe, First Secretary of the Western Siberian Krai, must
have subsequently made the request to which Mironov refers,
though Eikhe's specific request has not been located.

Anti-Soviet Conspiracies

No transcript of the June 1937 Plenum has been published. However, Iurii Zhukov quotes extensively from some archival transcript materials. We also have a "konspekt" (synopsis) of the remarks Ezhov made. It is dated June 23, which would make Ezhov's
remarks the first report of the Plenum. Ezhov's report was extremely alarming. It begins as follows:

> During the last three months the NKVD has
> uncovered a series of fascist anti-Soviet formations
> of former Trotskyist, Rights, S-Rs, and others. The
> most important of these anti-Soviet organizations
> are the following:
>
> a) The military-fascist conspiracy headed by
> leading commanders of the Red Army –
> Tukhachevsky, Gamarnik, Iakir, Uborevich, Kork,
> Eideman, and others.
>
> b) The Right-Fascist conspiracy within the NKVD,
> headed by Iagoda.
>
> c) The powerful espionage organization "POV"
> [=Polish Military Organization] headed by
> Unshlikht, Loganovskii, Doletskii and others.
>
> d) the Polish group of National-Democrats in
> Belorussia, headed by Goloded and Cherviakov.
>
> e) An anti-Soviet Right-Trotskyist group in the
> Azov-Chernmor'e and Ordzhonikidze oblasts
> headed by Sheboldaev, Pivovarov, Larin and others,
> united not only with Trotskyists and Rights but also

with powerful anti-Soviet Cossack and rebel partisan formations.

f) An anti-Soviet Right-Trotskyist group in Eastern Siberia headed by the First Secretary of the krai committee Razumov.

g) A Right anti-Soviet group in the Ural region headed by the First Secretary of the Sverdlovsk oblast' committee Kabakov.

h) An anti-Soviet Right-fascist group in the Western oblast' headed by the oblast' secretary Rumiantsev.

i) A very powerful Right-Trotskyist espionage organization in the Far East, headed by the Chairman of the krai executive committee Krutov, by Shmidt, and others.

j) A strong organization of Rights in Western Siberia which has united rebel partisan cadre among the special settlers [exiles].

k) An anti-Soviet Cossack organization in Orenburg oblast which has united Cossack and insurgent cadre and is tied to the ROVS [anticommunist White Russian émigré group] headed by the Chairman of the executive committee Vasil'ev and the Chairman of the City Soviet Kashirin.

l) A Right-Trotskyist anti-Soviet sabotage group in the People's Commissariat of Agriculture and the People's Commissariat of Soviet Farms.

The above is a list of only the most important groups.

Besides these, in almost all krais and oblasts there have been uncovered anti-Soviet formations in a bloc with the Rights, Trotskyists, Zinovievists, S-Rs, Mensheviks, and others. (Petrov & Iansen 293-4)

The first day of the June 1937 Plenum also saw proposals to exclude 7 sitting CC members and candidates for "lack of political trustworthiness." During the remaining Plenum sessions a further 19 members and candidates were expelled for "treason and active counterrevolutionary activity." These last 19 were to be arrested by the NKVD. Including the 10 members expelled on similar charges before the Plenum by a poll of the CC members (including those military commanders already tried, convicted, and executed), this meant that 36 of the 120 CC members and candidates as of May 1 had been removed from office.

Elections

Iakovlev and Molotov criticized the failure of Party leaders to organize for independent Soviet elections. Molotov stressed the need to move even honored revolutionaries out of the way if they were unprepared for the tasks of the day. He emphasized that Soviet officials were not "second-class workers" (persons of little importance). Evidently some Party leaders were treating them as such.

According to the agenda of the CC Plenum that has survived Iakovlev spoke on June 27. He exposed and criticized the failure of First Secretaries to hold secret elections for Party posts, relying instead on appointment. He emphasized that Party members who were elected delegates to the Soviets were not to be placed under the discipline of Party groups *outside* the Soviets and told how to vote. They were *not* to be told how to vote by their Party superiors, such as the First Secretaries. They were to be independent of them. And Iakovlev referred in the strongest terms to the need to "recruit from the very rich reserve of new cadre to replace those who had become rotten or bureaucratized." All these statements constituted an explicit attack on the First Secretaries. (Zhukov, Inoi 424-7; Tainy, 39-40, quoting from archival documents)

The Constitution was finally outlined and the date of the first elections was set for December 12, 1937. The Stalin leadership again urged the benefits of fighting bureaucracy and building ties to the masses.

However, all this followed the shocking, unprecedented, summary expulsion from the CC of 26 members, 19 of whom were directly charged with treason and counter-revolutionary activity. (Zhukov, Inoi 430)

Perhaps most revealing is the following remark by Stalin, as quoted by Zhukov:

> At the end of the discussion, when the subject was the search for a more dispassionate method of counting ballots, [Stalin] remarked that in the West, thanks to a multiparty system, this problem did not exist. Immediately thereafter he suddenly uttered a phrase that sounded very strange in a meeting of this kind: "We do not have different political parties. Fortunately or <u>unfortunately, we have only one party</u>." [Zhukov's emphasis] And then he proposed, but only as a temporary measure, to use for the purpose of dispassionate supervision of elections representatives of all existing societal organizations **except for the Bolshevik Party**... The challenge to the Party autocracy had been issued. (Zhukov, Inoi 430-1; Tainy 38)

The Bolshevik Party was in severe crisis, and it was impossible to expect that events would unroll smoothly. It was the worst possible atmosphere during which to prepare for the adoption of democratic -- secret, universal and contested -- elections.

Evidently Eikhe, and then a number of other First Secretaries, approached Stalin and the Politburo after the plenum and asked for authority to deal with conspiracies, rebellions, and revolts in their areas. This must have been when he made his formal request for special power, as outlined in the report by NKVD man Mironov that we have quoted above.

> Protocol #51 of the meeting of the Politburo VKP(b)
>
> 66. On the discovery of counterrevolutionary insurrectionist organizations among exiled kulaks in Western Siberia
>
> Decision of *28 June 1937*

Item #66. Re: The uncovering of a counterrevolutionary, insurrectionary organization among deported kulaks in Western Siberia.

1. We consider it necessary to apply the supreme penalty to all activists belonging to this insurrectionary organization of deported kulaks.

2. In order to speed up the review of cases, troikas to be formed consisting of Comrade Mironov (chairman), head of the NKVD for Western Siberia, Comrade Barkov, public prosecutor (*prokuror*) for Western Siberia, and Comrade Eikhe, secretary of the Western-Siberian Territorial Committee.

Secretary of the CC. (Getty & Naumov, 469; Lubianka 1937-1938 232 No.110)

Zhukov thinks that Eikhe may have been acting on behalf of an informal group of First Secretaries, for after Eikhe several other First Secretaries met with Stalin. They probably also demanded the extraordinary powers that they were granted shortly afterward: the authority to form *troikas,* groups of three officials, to combat widespread conspiracies against the Soviet government in their area.[1] These troikas were given the power of execution without appeal. Numerical limits – not "quotas," as many anticommunist scholars dishonestly claim, maximum, not minimum, numbers -- for those to be shot and others to be imprisoned on the sole authority of these *troikas* were set. When those were exhausted, the First Secretaries asked for, and often received, higher limits. (Getty, Excesses 129; Zhukov, Inoi 435)

On July 2, 1937, shortly after the conclusion of the plenum, the Politburo – Stalin and those closest to him – issued the following decree:

94. On anti-Soviet elements.

---

[1] The order for setting up a troika in Eikhe's Western Siberian region exists. Eikhe's request has not been found, but he must have made such a request, either in writing or orally. See Zhukov, Repressii 23, n. 60; Getty, Excesses 127, n. 64.

The following telegram is to be sent to secretaries of regional and territorial committees and to the CCs of national Communist parties:

"It has been observed that a large part of the former kulaks and criminals deported at one time from various oblasts to Northern and Siberian districts and then having returned to their regions at the expiration of their period of exile – are the chief instigators of all sorts of anti-Soviet crimes and sabotage, both in the kolkhozy and sovkhozy as well as in transport and in certain branches of industry.

The CC VKP(b) recommends to all secretaries of oblast' and krai organizations and to all oblast', krai, and republic representatives of the NKVD that they register all kulaks and criminals who have returned to their native homes in order that the most hostile among them be immediately arrested and shot through an administrative study of their cases by a troika, and that the remaining, less active but nevertheless hostile elements be listed and exiled to regions [raiony] according to the directions of the NKVD.

The CC VKP(b) recommends that the names of the staffs of the troikas and also the number of those subject to execution and the number subject to exile, be presented to the CC within five days.

To Com. Ezhov, the secretaries of the oblast' and krai party committees, and to the CCs of the national Communist parties. (Lubianka 1937-1938 234-235 No. 114) [2]

---

[2] Online at http://www.memo.ru/history/document/pbkulaki.htm A slightly different translation is in Getty & Naumov, Doc. 169, 470-471.

The mass repressions of Ezhov, also known as the *Ezhovshchina* and, prejudicially, as "the Great Terror," were about to commence.

Chapter 6. Causes of the Repression

Who were the targets of these draconian trials-by-troika?

In common with virtually all historians of the USSR Iurii Zhukov largely discounts the existence of real conspiracies. He believes they must have been *lishentsy*, the very people whose citizenship rights, including franchise, had recently been restored and whose votes potentially posed the greatest danger to the First Secretaries' continuance in power. This may indeed have been one of the motives of some of the regional Party leaders. But it should not simply be assumed, and as yet we have no evidence to support it.

Other historians claim that this mass repression was led by Stalin, who was trying to kill anybody who might be disloyal, a "Fifth Column," if the Soviet Union were invaded. (While that was the goal of the leadership, including Stalin, the mass repressions by the troikas were organized by Ezhov. They were not part of Stalin's effort. The Moscow Trials and their outcome, and later the trials, sentences and executions that put an end to Ezhov's conspiracy, were a part of Stalin's effort.) Still others claim that Stalin was out to murder any and all possible rivals, or was paranoid, or simply mad. There is no evidence to support these notions.

In fact the reason for the campaign of repression stands out clearly in all the evidence we have – and we have a lot of evidence. The subversive activities and rebellions that Mironov, Eikhe, and other regional Party leaders and NKVD men reported were a logical consequence of the conspiracies that had been gradually discovered since the assassination of Sergei M. Kirov over the previous 2 ½ years:

* The Kirov murder of December 1, 1934.

* The Kremlin Affair conspiracy, uncovered during 1935.

* Those disclosed in the First Moscow Trial of August 1936, of Zinoviev, Kamenev, their co-conspirators, and some Trotskyists who were collaborating with the Germans.

* Those disclosed in the Second Moscow Trial of January 1937 of a far-flung Trotskyist conspiracy in league with Germany, Japan, England, France, and homegrown Russian fascists.

* Genrikh Iagoda's NKVD conspiracy, uncovered beginning in April 1937 – part of the Rightists' conspiracy disclosed at the January 1937 trial and the subject of the Third Moscow Trial of March 1938.

* The "May Days" revolt in Barcelona, at the beginning of May 1937.

* The Tukhachevsky Affair military conspiracy, uncovered in April, May, and June 1937.

Before Nikita Khrushchev's "Secret Speech" to the XX Party Congress of the CPSU on February 25, 1956, few anticommunist specialists in Soviet studies doubted the real existence of these conspiracies. Only the Trotskyist movement, faithful to their murdered leader, claimed that these conspiracies were fabrications by Stalin.

This changed after Khrushchev's speech. Virtually all anticommunists, as well as most communists and, of course, all Trotskyists, chose to believe Khrushchev's allegations against Stalin. It followed from what Khrushchev implied in 1956, and from what his supporters claimed even more stridently at the XXII Party Congress in October 1961 that the defendants in all the Moscow Trials, plus the Tukhachevsky Affair defendants, had all been innocent victims of a frame-up. Mikhail Gorbachev's lieutenants made the same assertions.

Since Khrushchev's day the consensus among professional students of Soviet history has conformed to the Khrushchev-Gorbachev position: there were no conspiracies, all were inventions by Stalin. This is all false.

There has never been any evidence that any of these conspiracies were frame-ups or that any of the defendants were innocent. Just the opposite is the case. The evidence is overwhelming that Kirov was indeed murdered by the clandestine Zinovievist group and that Zinoviev and Kamenev were involved in the group's activities, including Kirov's murder. Trotskyists and Trotsky himself were also implicated. (Furr, Kirov)

We have a great deal of evidence that the conspiracies alleged in all three Moscow Trials were real and that all the defendants were guilty of at least what they confessed to. In some cases, we can now prove that defendants were guilty of crimes that they did not reveal to the Prosecution. We also have a great deal of evidence on the Tukhachevsky Affair. All of it supports the hypothesis that the defendants were guilty as charged. (Furr Amalgams)

The evidence that all these conspiracies did in fact exist allows us to view the Ezhov mass repressions of July 1937 to October-November 1938 objectively and in their proper context.

It was logical for the Stalin leadership to accept the claims of regional NKVD and Party leaders that serious conspiracies and violent insurgencies existed throughout the country. Some of the most senior military commanders in the country had just admitted to plotting a *coup d'état* and, failing that, to sabotage the country's defines in the event of invasion by Germany and/or Japan, with which enemy regimes they were coordinating their actions. Genrikh Iagoda, until recently the head of the NKVD, was confessing that he too had been a secret oppositionist implicated in the murder of Sergei Kirov and in plots to get rid of Stalin and his associates.

Tukhachevsky and the rest had ties with the bloc of Rights, Trotskyists, and other oppositionists too. Like Radek and Piatakov, Trotsky's senior lieutenants, Tukhachevsky and some of his co-defendants testified that Trotsky was collaborating with the Germans. Defendants at the January 1937 Moscow trial had revealed that German agents and Russian fascists were active in anti-Soviet conspiracies in the Kuzbass coal fields.

Denial

Since Khrushchev's day academic Soviet history has been committed to a demonized view of Stalin. We have called this the "anti-Stalin paradigm." Western historians of the USSR have accepted Khrushchev's supposed "revelations" as unproblematically true despite the fact that Khrushchev never gave any evidence for his charges against Stalin and in fact withheld evidence from Party researchers who asked for it.

The main evidentiary basis for Robert Conquest's book *The Great Terror* and for works by dissidents such as Roi Medvedev's *Let History Judge* and Alexander Nekrich' *June 1941*, was the Khrushchev-era "revelations." Western historians' accounts of the Stalin period continue to rely heavily on Khrushchev-era accounts.

Some years ago Vladimir L. Bobrov and I studied the tenth chapter of Stephen F. Cohen's famous book *Bukharin and the Bolshevik Revolution*. In this chapter Cohen traces Bukharin's life from 1930 until his trial and execution in March 1938. Through the use of primary source evidence from former Soviet archives we showed that every fact-claim Cohen makes in this chapter that in any way alleges wrong-doing by Stalin is false. Cohen relied on Khrushchev-era sources – and all of them have proven to be lies. The result is that Chapter 10 of this celebrated book is entirely false. (Furr & Bobrov, Cohen)

From the time of the Bolshevik Revolution in 1917 the study of Soviet history has developed as an adjunct of political anticommunism. It has always had a dual character: that of discovering what happened, and that of defaming Stalin, the Soviet Union, and communism generally.

The result is that academic historiography of the Soviet Union is rarely if ever objective. It has "sacred cows," tenets that are never questioned. This is the "anti-Stalin paradigm." Academic historians of the USSR are pressured to conform to this paradigm, or at least not openly violate it.

Chief among the tenets of the anti-Stalin paradigm is that all the Moscow Trials, plus the Tukhachevsky Affair, were frame-ups. Today we know that this is false. An objective study of the evidence now available from former Soviet archives, from the Trotsky archives, and elsewhere, proves that these conspiracies did indeed exist.

But the political demands that constrain the academic field of Soviet history require the denial that *any* of these conspiracies existed! According to this view – the only one officially permitted in the field – the Moscow Trials defendants, Tukhachevsky & Co., and all other alleged conspirators were forced to confess and then executed, an act attributed to Stalin alone, for whatever reason you like only *not* for any real conspiracy to overthrow the Soviet government and Party leadership and ally with the Axis – that is, to act as a Fifth Column.

This false paradigm deprives academic historians of the ability to understand the conspiracy trials. It robs them of the ability to understand the context for the Ezhov-era mass repressions. They conclude that the reasons for these repressions are inscrutable because they have declared that the previous conspiracies could not have existed.

The Threat Was Real

On the evidence now available we can confidently state that these conspiracies did exist. Archival documents show that the central Party leadership, Stalin and the Politburo, were constantly receiving very credible police accounts of conspiracies, including transcripts of confessions and details of NKVD investigations. Certainly Stalin and others in Moscow believed these conspiracies existed. On the evidence we now have it appears that at least some of the alleged conspiracies really did exist. (Zhukov, KP Nov. 13 02; Inoi, Ch. 18; Repressii 23)

We also possess a number of accounts of these conspiracies from beyond the borders of the USSR (and thus beyond any power of the Soviet prosecution or NKVD to fabricate them). Examples of such accounts include the following:

* Grigory Tokaev, *Comrade X.* Tokaev describes a widespread secret anti-Stalin conspiracy involving several figures expelled from the Party, tried and executed for such conspiracies, such as Sheboldaev and Enukidze. (6) Sheboldaev was expelled on June 25, 1937, during the June 1937 Plenum. Avel' Enukidze had been arrested much earlier and, by April 1937, was already confessing to his own involvement in the conspiracy. Tokaev names others

and also confirms the existence of a military-civilian conspiracy led by a military man, "Comrade X."

* A. Svetlanin -- real name N.N. Likhachev -- *Dal'nevostochnyi Zagovor* (The Far Eastern Conspiracy). Likhachev became editor of the CIA-sponsored Soviet émigré journal *Posev*. He confirms the military conspiracy in the Far Eastern Army and its links to civilian conspirators. One of the latter was Ivan Rumiantsev, First Secretary of the Western Oblast', also expelled from the Party during the June 1937 Plenum.[1]

* Genrikh S. Liushkov, an NKVD general who defected to the Japanese in June 1938. Liushkov privately told his Japanese handlers that there really were military conspiracies in the Far East with connections to the Rights through Aleksei Rykov, who with Bukharin was a major defendant in the Third Moscow Trial.

* Discoveries in the Harvard Trotsky Archive confirm the existence of the bloc of oppositionists referred to in all the Moscow Trials.

* American engineers John D. Littlepage and Carroll G. Holmes confirmed sabotage by Piatakov and I.N. Smirnov, or by those under their guidance, consistent with the charges at the second Moscow trial of January 1937.

I have discussed these last two points in detail in *Trotsky's 'Amalgams'.*

Accounts like these confirm and supplement the large amount of evidence from Soviet sources that we now possess. The sheer volume of police documentation concerning such conspiracies, only a little of which has yet been published, argues strongly against any notion that all of it could have been fabricated. Furthermore, Stalin's annotations on these documents make it clear that he believed they were accurate. (Getty, Excesses 131-4; Lubianka 1937-1938)

---

[1] In the early 1980s I tried to verify this account by writing to persons who had known Likhachev. Prof. Nikolai Andreyev, of Cambridge University (now deceased), wrote me two letters telling me of his close friendship with Likhachev/Svetlanin/Frolov; of how highly he thought of his trustworthiness.

The NKVD and regional Party leadership – however compromised by the very recent revelations that some of their number had been active in these conspiracies too – must have appeared to be the only force that Soviet power could rely upon. It did not become clear until much later that Ezhov too was conspiring with foreign powers to overthrow the government and Party leadership, and was using massive executions of innocent people to stir up resentment.

Getty summarizes the hopeless situation in this way:

> Stalin was not yet willing to retreat from contested elections, and on 2 July 1937 *Pravda* no doubt disappointed the regional secretaries by publishing the first installment of the new electoral rules, enacting and enforcing contested, universal, secret ballot elections. But ... [t]he very same day the electoral law was published, the Politburo approved the launching of a mass operation against precisely the elements the local leaders had complained about ... (Excesses 126)

Getty appears to think that Stalin gave the local party leaders the right to arrest and kill or deport those who might oppose them in elections. But there is no evidence of any such thing. There *is* evidence of conspiracies, some in collaboration with Germany or Japan.

At first the Politburo tried to limit the campaign of repression by ordering that it be completed within *five days*. Something convinced or compelled them to extend the period to *four months*_-- August 5-15 to December 5-15. Was it the large numbers of those arrested? The conviction that the Party faced a widespread set of conspiracies and a huge internal threat? This explanation seems likely, though we can't be sure.

But this was exactly the period during which the electoral campaign was to take place. Even though the Politburo continued preparation for the contested elections, with rules about how voters were to indicate their choices, and how officials should handle runoff elections, local officials actually controlled the repression. They could determine what opposition, if any, to the Party – which meant, in great part, to themselves – would be considered "loyal," and what would lead to repression. (Getty, Excesses, *passim.*; Zhukov, Inoi 435)

Primary documents show that Stalin and the central Politburo leadership were convinced that anti-Soviet conspirators were active and had to be dealt with. This is what the regional Party leaders had asserted during the February-March Plenum. At that time the Stalin leadership had minimized this danger and had kept focusing attention back to the preparations for new elections and the replacement of "bureaucratized" leaders with new ones.

By the June Plenum the First Secretaries were in a position to say, in effect: "We told you so. We were right, and you were wrong. Furthermore, we are *still* right – dangerous conspirators are still active, ready to use the electoral campaign in their attempt to raise revolt against the Soviet government." Was this how it happened? It seems plausible, but we cannot be sure.

Stalin and the central leadership could have had no idea how deep these conspiracies extended. Nor could they know what Nazi Germany or fascist Japan might do. On June 2 Stalin had told the expanded Military Soviet meeting that the Tukhachevsky group had given the Red Army's operational plan to the German General Staff. This meant that the Japanese, who were bound in a military alliance (the "Axis") and an anti-communist political alliance (the "Anti-Comintern Pact") with fascist Italy and Nazi Germany, would doubtless have it too.

Stalin had told the military leaders that the plotters wanted to make the USSR into "another Spain" – form a Fifth Column in coordination with an invading fascist army. Faced with this terrible and imminent danger, the Soviet leadership was determined to react decisively. (Stalin, Vystuplenie)

Much evidence suggests that the central (Stalin) leadership wanted both to restrain the "troika" repressions demanded by the First Secretaries and to continue to implement the new Constitution's secret and contested elections. From July 5 to 11 most First

Secretaries followed Eikhe's lead in sending in precise figures of those whom they wanted to suppress – by execution (category 1) or imprisonment (category 2). Then...

> [S]uddenly on 12 July, Deputy NKVD Commissar
> M.P. Frinovskii sent an urgent telegram to all local
> police agencies: "Do not begin the operation to
> repress former kulaks. I repeat, do not begin."
> (Getty, Excesses 127-8)

NKVD Evidence of Conspiracies Sent to Stalin

For the next year or more the Stalin leadership was flooded with reports of conspiracies and revolts from all over the USSR. A large number of these have been published (in Russian). Undoubtedly a great many more remain unpublished. The principal collections of published documents for the years of the mass repressions, 1937 and 1938, are these:

* *Lubianka. Stalin i Glavnoe Upravlenie Gosbezopasnosti NKVD. 1937-1938.* Moscow: "Materik," 2004. (Lubianka 1937-1938)

* *Lubianka. Sovetskaia elita na stalinskoi golgofe 1937-1938. Dokumenty.* Moscow: Mezhdunarodnyi Fond "Demokratiia." 2011. (Lubianka Golgofa)

* *Lubianka. Stalin i NKVD-NKGB-GUKR "Smersh." 1939 – mart 1946.* Moscow: MDF, 2006 (Lubianka 1939-1946)

The first two volumes contain dozens of reports sent to Stalin by the NKVD – meaning, by Ezhov. They include many confessions of leading Party officials and NKVD men concerning their involvement in anti-Soviet conspiracies. The final volume contains a number of confessions and interrogation-confessions from 1939. We will carefully examine two of these documents in future chapters: Mikhail Frinovskii's statement to NKVD chief Lavrentii Beria of April 11, 1939, and Nikolai Ezhov's interrogation-confession of April 26, 1939.

A number of these documents are reproduced from copies studied and marked up by Stalin himself. These remarks give us insight into how Stalin interpreted the documents. In every case it is clear that Stalin studied their contents very carefully and took them very seriously. He asked questions, often very probing ones, and made suggestions for further investigation based on the contents of the interrogations and confessions presented to him. These remarks show that Stalin was not fabricating these reports – he was *studying* them. Stalin was trying to find out what was going on, what the extent of the dangerous conspiracies was.

The editor of the second volume above is V.N. Khaustov, a very anti-Stalin researcher and one of the compilers of several important document collections. According to Khaustov, Stalin believed these reports.

> And the most frightening thing was that Stalin
> made his decisions on the basis of confessions that
> were the result of the inventions of certain
> employees of the organs of state security. Stalin's
> reactions attest to the fact that he took these
> confessions completely seriously. (Lubianka
> Golgofa 6)

What is important here is this:

* Khaustov admits the existence of a major conspiracy by Ezhov and concedes that Stalin was deceived by him. Ezhov admits as much in the confessions of his that we now have.

* Khaustov admits that Stalin acted in good faith on the basis of evidence presented to him by Ezhov, much of which may, or must, have been false.

It is important to ideologically anticommunist researchers that these mass murders be seen as Stalin's plan and intention. Khaustov is honest enough to admit that the evidence does not bear this out. Some of the confessional and investigative documents Ezhov sent on to Stalin and the Soviet leadership must have been falsifications. But in reality Khaustov has no idea which were fabrications and which were not.

These documents, and Stalin's comments on them, are rarely discussed by mainstream historians of the Soviet Union when they are considering the mass repressions of 1937-1938. They dismantle the "anti-Stalin paradigm." They show Stalin reacting thoughtfully and attentively to the reports sent to him. Of course this is what any student would expect -- unless he or she were blinded by the "anti-Stalin paradigm."

Iurii Zhukov suggests that after Eikhe got these special powers for Western Siberia the other First Secretaries asked Stalin for the same powers, and received them. Evidently there was a connection between this campaign of repressions, carried out as a virtual war against rebellious anti-Soviet forces throughout the country, and the cancellation of the competitive elections that had been stipulated under the new 1936 Soviet Constitution.

Stalin and his supporters in the central Soviet government and Party fought for such elections but failed to win the Central Committee to approve them. Zhukov has traced the final decision not to hold such elections to October 11, 1937. He also located a draft or sample ballot for contested elections — a ballot never used but preserved in a Soviet archive.

Chapter 7. The Course of the Repressions

This chapter discusses the major events of the Ezhov mass repressions of July 1937-November 1938. We have determined what events to discuss by consulting the following work:

* N.G. Okhotin and A.B. Roginskii, "'The Great Terror': 1937-1938. A Short Chronology." (Khronika)[1]

Roginskii is the chairman of the "Memorial Society," a fanatically anticommunist organization in Russia. Okhotin is a principal researcher in the same organization.

Nothing published by "Memorial" can make any claim to objectivity; everything is heavily biased. These authors would never exclude anything that would show Stalin and the Stalin government in a negative light.

One important aspect of this document's bias is what it omits. The chronology ignores all the context and all the evidence coming to the Politburo from the NKVD around the country. It lists the decrees, orders, and events without any reference to the documentary evidence that were the basis for these events. We listed three of the collections of this material in the last chapter.

The "Memorial" researchers assume that all the alleged conspiracies were frame-ups, that the defendants at these trials were innocent, and that no conspiracies existed. This is the logical fallacy of *petitio principii* – "begging the question" or "assuming that which is to be proven."[2] This fallacy is very common in mainstream historiography of the Stalin period. It follows that they consider all those accused and convicted of anti-Soviet conspiracies to be "vic-

---

[1] This long document is online and thus lacks pagination. I have divided it into 20 "pages."

[2] See https://en.wikipedia.org/wiki/Begging_the_question

tims" and their punishment "repression" – terms not used for the conviction and punishment of criminals.

Since the "Memorial" people believe all the conspiracies alleged during the Stalin years were frame-ups, the Okhotin-Roginskii chronology begins with March 1936, the prelude to the First Moscow Trial of August 1936, and includes references to all the Moscow Trials. Here we will define the period of mass repression as beginning in July 1937, the month the troikas were formed and at the end of which Operational Order No. 00447 was issued, and ending in November 1938, when Ezhov resigned and a series of resolutions suddenly stopped all the mechanism of special repression.

During this period, July 1937 through November 1938, Khronika lists 107 events. Only a few of these events deal with actions outside the normal bounds of security operations. Those are the ones we will examine here. They are:

* Operational Order of the NKVD No. (OO NKVD) 00439 – German Operation July 25, 1937 (Khronika 9)

* OO NKVD 00447 July 31 1937 (Khronika 9)

* OO NKVD 00485 Polish Operation August 11 1937 (Khronika 10)

* OO NKVD 00486 – Wives and children August 15 1937 (Khronika 10)

First we will examine two other issues: That of the "lists" (Khronika 5) and that of "limits." A truthful account of these topics is essential to any accurate understanding of the Ezhov mass repressions. This is the reason that accounts of both of them are falsified by most academic experts on Soviet history.

The Lists

Khrushchev:

> The vicious practice was condoned of having the
> NKVD prepare lists of persons whose cases were
> under the jurisdiction of the Military Collegium **and
> whose sentences were prepared in advance**.
> Yezhov would send these lists to Stalin personally

for his approval of the proposed punishment. In
1937-1938, 383 such lists containing the names of
many thousands of party, Soviet, Komsomol, Army
and economic workers were sent to Stalin. He
approved these lists.

These lists exist, and have been edited and published, first on CD
and now on the Internet. They are titled the "Stalin 'Shooting'
Lists." Some writers dishonestly call them "death warrants." These
are both tendentious, inaccurate names, for these were not lists of
persons "to be shot" at all.

Following Khrushchev, the anti-Stalin editors of these lists do in
fact call the lists "sentences prepared in advance." But their own
research disproves this claim. The lists give the sentences that the
NKVD *recommended* the prosecution would seek if the individual
were convicted – that is, the sentence the Prosecution would ask
the court to apply.

In reality these were lists sent to Stalin (and other Politburo or
Secretariat members) for "review" – *rassmotrenie* – a word that is
used many times in the introduction to the lists.[3] Many people on
these lists were not convicted, or were convicted of a lesser of-
fense, and so not shot. One example is that of A.V. Snegov, whom
Khrushchev mentions by name in his "Secret Speech." Snegov is on
the lists at least twice:

* At http://stalin.memo.ru/spiski/pg13026.htm No. 383;

* At http://stalin.memo.ru/spiski/pg05245.htm No. 133.

In this last reference Snegov is specifically put into "1st Category,"
meaning: recommended sentence of death in the event of conviction. A brief summary of the Prosecutor's evidence against him is
provided. There was a lot of evidence against Snegov! Nevertheless Snegov was not sentenced to death but instead to a long term
in a labor camp. He survived to be freed by Khrushchev and to
have been an honored guest in the audience at Khrushchev's infamous "Secret Speech."

---

[3] The introduction is at http://www.memo.ru/history/vkvs/images/intro1.htm The next
quotation is also from this source.

According to the editors of these lists "many" people whose names are on them were not in fact executed, and some were freed.

> For example, a selective study of the list for the Kuibyshev oblast' signed on September 29, 1938 shows that not a single person on this list was convicted by the VKVS (the Military Collegium of the Supreme Court), and a significant number of the cases were dismissed altogether.

So Khrushchev knew that Stalin was not "sentencing" anybody but rather reviewing the lists in case he had any objections. We can be certain that Khrushchev knew this because the note of February 3, 1954, to Khrushchev from S. N. Kruglov, Minister of Internal Affairs (MVD) has survived. It says nothing about "sentences prepared in advance," but gives the truth:

> These lists were compiled in 1937 and 1938 by the NKVD of the USSR and presented to the CC of the ACP(b) **for review** right away.

The Prosecutor went to trial not only with evidence but with a sentence to recommend to the judges in case of conviction.

It appears that the names of Party members, but not of non-Party members, were sent on for review. The disingenuous Introduction notes that those signing the lists comprised "not all the Politburo members but only those of its members who were closest to Stalin." But the evidence suggests that it was the members of the Party Secretariat rather than the Politburo to whom the lists were submitted. Even the editors note that Ezhov – a member of the Secretariat but not of the Politburo – signed "as a secretary of the Central Committee."

We do not know whether additional information – for example, evidence, summaries of testimony against those named on the lists, etc. – was sent to the Secretariat along with the lists. As we saw in the last chapter, during the period in question Stalin was receiving reports, often very lengthy and detailed ones, from Ezhov on an almost daily basis. That means we know that Stalin and others in the Secretariat possessed other materials to consult when reviewing the names on these lists. The lists were part of a complex of information and cannot be objectively understood without taking this context into account.

It is obvious too that the lists were a kind of safety mechanism. If Stalin had received no lists, or if reports were presented to him only in oral format, there would be no such lists. Then we would know less about what was going on. Also, anticommunists would not have these lists to present, in a decontextualized manner, as supposed "evidence" of Stalin's purported "murders."

Khrushchev concealed the fact that not Stalin but he himself was one of the persons deeply involved in selecting the persons for inclusion on these lists and choosing the category of punishment proposed for them. Khrushchev mentions that the NKVD prepared the lists. But he does not mention the fact that the NKVD acted together with the Party leadership, and that a great many of the names on these lists – perhaps more than from any other region of the USSR – originated in the areas under Khrushchev's own authority.

Until January 1938 Khrushchev was First Secretary of the Party in Moscow and Moscow oblast' (province). After that he was First Secretary in the Ukraine. His letter to Stalin asking for permission to shoot 8500 people is dated July 10, 1937, the same date as the first of the "shooting lists" from Moscow.

> "CC ACP(b) – to comrade Stalin J.V.

> I report that we have counted a total of 41,305 criminal and kulak elements who have served their sentences and settled in Moscow city and province.

> Of those there are 33,436 criminal elements **materials at hand give us the basis to put 6,500 criminals in Category 1** [to be shot – GF], and 26,396 in Category 2 [to be exiled - GF]. Of this number, for orientation purposes in the city of Moscow there are 1,500 in Category 1 and 5,272 in Category 2.

> We have calculated there are 7,869 kulaks who have served their sentences and settled in Moscow

city and oblast' Materials at hand give us the basis
to put 2,000 from this group into Category 1 and
5,869 in Category 2.

We request that a commission be confirmed,
consisting of comrades Redens, head of the UNKVD
for the Moscow oblast'; Maslov, assistant
prosecutor of the Moscow oblast', and Khrushchev,
N.S. – Secretary of the Moscow Committee and
Moscow City Committee, with the right, when
necessary, to be replaced by A.A. Volkov – second
secretary of the Moscow City Committee.

Secretary of the M[oscow] C[ommittee] of the
ACP(b) –

(N. Khrushchev)." July 10, 1937.[4]

Getty (Excesses, 127) cites Khrushchev's request for 41,000 people in both categories:

In Moscow, First Secretary Nikita Khrushchev knew
that he needed to repress exactly 41,805 kulaks and
criminals. Nearly all of the submissions from the
forty provinces and republics responding to Stalin's
telegram were in such exact figures.[5]

In the same letter Khrushchev also confirms his own participation
in the troika responsible for selecting these names, along with the
head of the directorate of the NKVD for Moscow, S.F. Redens, and
the assistant prosecutor K.I. Maslov (Khrushchev does admit that
"when necessary" he was replaced by the second secretary A.A.
Volkov).

Volkov served as second secretary of the Moscow Region of the
AUCP(b) only till the beginning of August 1937, when he left to

---

[4] *Trud* June 4, 1992; republished in *Molotov, Malenkov, Kaganovich. 1957.* Moscow: Mezhdunarodnyi Fond "Demokratiia," 1998 p. 747, n. 22; *Tragediia sovetskoi derevni t. 5 kn. 1.
1937.* Moscow: ROSSPEN 2004, 324. Online at http://istmat.info/node/33727

[5] The printed source in the previous note gives the total as 41305; Getty writes 41,805. This
must be from the same document so someone has copied incorrectly.

serve as First Secretary of the Belorussian party. After that he was no longer Khrushchev's subordinate, which may have saved his life. Maslov remained Procuror (prosecutor) of the Moscow oblast' (province) until November 1937. In 1938 he was arrested and was executed in March 1939, after having been found guilty of subversive counterrevolutionary activity. The same fate befell K.I. Mamonov who at first occupied Maslov's position and was later shot the same day as Maslov.

Nor did Redens escape punishment. He was arrested in November 1938 as a member of a "Polish diversionist-espionage group," tried and sentenced, and shot on January 21, 1940. This was precisely when Nikolai Ezhov and many of his henchmen in the NKVD were tried and executed. In fact Jansen and Petrov describe Redens as one of "Ezhov's men." During the years of the "thaw" Redens was rehabilitated at Khrushchev's insistence but by such crude violations of legal procedures that in 1988 an attempt was made to reverse Redens' rehabilitation – at a time when a huge wave of rehabilitations was under way!

This means that with the exception of Volkov all of Khrushchev's closest co-workers who took part in repressions in Moscow and Moscow oblast' were severely punished. How did Khrushchev manage to escape the same punishment? The answer to this puzzle remains to be uncovered.

The Limits

The Politburo set limits on the numbers of persons the Party leaders and NKVD could execute and imprison in the campaigns against insurgents and conspirators.

> Order No. 00447 established limits [*limity*] rather than quotas, maximums, not minimums. ... As we have seen, for years Stalin had been putting limits on mass executions by provincial leaders. If the Politburo had at this moment expected or wanted an open-ended terror, there would be no reason to call them 'limits' at all. The word's meaning was well known: it never meant 'quotas'. Reflecting Stalin's concern that locals might go out of control

> (or out of his control) Order No. 00447 twice
> warned that 'excesses' in local implementation of
> the operation were not permitted. (Getty, Fever
> 232-233)

Getty also emphasizes this fact in a recent book:

> One of the mysteries of the field [of Soviet history
> — GF] is how *limity* is routinely translated as
> "quotas." (Getty, Practicing 340 n. 109)

One writer who constantly translates "limity" as "quotas" is Oleg
Khlevniuk. Another is Timothy Snyder. Ideologically biased, anti-
communist writers *want* Stalin to have called for "quotas" so that
Stalin appears more bloodthirsty.

The Operational Orders of the NKVD

No. 00439 – the "German Operation" order July 25, 1937

Okhotin and Roginskii describe it as follows:

> Operational Order of the NKVD No. 439
> "Concerning the operation to repress German
> citizens suspected of espionage against the USSR"
> (primarily intended were those working in the
> defense industry and in transportation). Arrests
> began on July 29. Beginning in the autumn the
> operation gradually began to spread to some
> categories of Soviet Germans and other citizens
> accused of ties with Germany and espionage in
> Germany's behalf. (Khronika 9)

They go on to say that Order No. 00439 was abused to the extent
that 41,898 persons were sentenced to death under it. Okhotin and
Roginskii know how and why this happened – that this was
Ezhov's doing, not authorized by Stalin and the Politburo. Their
readers will not know this. We will discuss this in a future chapter.

No. 00447 – the "Kulak Operation" order July 31, 1937

After the June 1937 Plenum local NKVD chiefs were recalled to Moscow for conferences, after which Order No. 00447 was issued. This long, detailed instruction both expanded the kinds of people subject to repression (basically including priests, those who had previously opposed Soviet power, and criminals), and – usually – lowered the "limits" or numbers requested by the provincial secretaries.

Order No. 00447 is available in Russian in many places, and (in excerpt) also in English. This document authorizes action *only* against those involved in rebellions and criminal activities:

I. GROUPS SUBJECT TO PUNITIVE MEASURES.

1. Former kulaks who have returned home after having served their sentences **and who continue to carry out active, anti-Soviet sabotage**.

2. Former kulaks **who have escaped** from camps or from labor settlements, as well as kulaks who have been in hiding from dekulakization, **who carry out anti-Soviet activities.**

3. Former kulaks and socially dangerous elements who were members of insurrectionary, fascist, terroristic, and bandit formations who have served their sentences, **who have been in hiding from punishment, or who have escaped from places of confinement and renewed their anti-Soviet, criminal activities.**

4. Members of anti-Soviet parties (SRs, Georgian Mensheviks, Dashnaks, Mussavatists, Ittihadists, etc.), former Whites, gendarmes, bureaucrats, members of punitive expeditions, bandits, gang abettors, transferees, re-emigres, **who are in hiding from punishment, who have escaped from places of confinement, and who continue to carry out active anti-Soviet activities.**

5. Persons unmasked by investigators and **whose evidence is verified by materials obtained by**

investigative agencies and who are the most hostile and active members of Cossack-White Guard insurrectionary organizations slated for liquidation and fascist, terroristic, and espionage-saboteur counterrevolutionary formations. In addition, punitive measures are to be taken against elements of this category who are kept at the present under guard, whose cases have been fully investigated but not yet considered by the judicial organs.

6. **The most active anti-Soviet elements** from former kulaks, members of punitive expeditions, bandits, Whites, sectarian activists, church officials, and others, who are presently held in prisons, camps, labor settlements, and colonies **and who continue to carry out in those places their active anti-Soviet sabotage.**

7. Criminals (bandits, robbers, recidivist thieves, professional contraband smugglers, recidivist swindlers, cattle and horse thieves) **who are carrying out criminal activities and who are associated with the criminal underworld.** In addition, punitive measures are to be taken against elements of this category who are kept at the present under guard, whose cases have been fully investigated but not yet considered by the judicial organs.

8. Criminal elements in camps and labor settlements **who are carrying out criminal activities in them.**

9. All of the groups enumerated above, to be found at present in the countryside —i.e., in kolkhozy, sovkhozy, on agricultural enterprises, as well as in the city—i.e., at industrial and trade enterprises, in transport, in Soviet institutions, and in

construction, are subject to punitive measures.
(Getty & Naumov, 474-5)

We have used boldface type to emphasize the fact that those at whom Order No. 00447 was aimed were not to be targeted or punished because of their identity or because of past activity but *solely for current criminal activity*. Ezhov and his men ignored these strictures.

Order 00447 continues by specifying two categories of punishment: death and imprisonment.

> II. CONCERNING THE PUNISHMENT TO BE
> IMPOSED ON THOSE SUBJECT TO PUNITIVE
> MEASURES AND THE NUMBER OF PERSONS
> SUBJECT TO PUNITIVE MEASURES.
>
> 1. All kulaks, criminals, and other anti-Soviet
> elements subject to punitive measures are broken
> down into two categories:
>
> a) To the first category belong all **the most active**
> of the above-mentioned elements. They are subject
> to immediate arrest and, after consideration of
> their case by the troikas, to be shot.
>
> b) To the second category belong all **the remaining
> less active but nonetheless hostile** elements.
> They are subject to arrest and to confinement in
> concentration camps for a term ranging from 8 to
> 10 years, while the most vicious and socially
> dangerous among them are subject to confinement
> for similar terms in prisons as determined by the
> troikas.

Limits were then established by region for the "limit" or maximum number of persons to be sentenced in each category.[6] A few examples:

---

[6] Both the Wikipedia article https://en.wikipedia.org/wiki/NKVD_Order_No._00447 and the article by Nicolas Werth in the "Online Encyclopedia of Mass Violence" use – dishonestly --

Region	First Category	Second Category	Total
Azerbaijan SSR	1,500	3,750	5,250
Armenian SSR	500	1,000	1,500
Belorussian SSR	2,000	10,000	12,000
Georgian SSR	2,000	3,000	5,000
Kirghiz SSR	250	500	750
Tadzhik SSR	500	1,300	1,800
Turkmen SSR	500	1,500	2,000

Treatment of families of those arrested is specified.

....4. The families of those sentenced in accordance with the first or second category are not as a rule subject to punitive measures. Exceptions to this include:

a) Families, members of which are capable of active anti-Soviet actions. Pursuant to the special decree by the three-man commission, members of such families are subject to being transferred to camps or labor settlements.

b) The families of persons punished in accordance with the first category, who live in border areas, are subject to expulsion beyond the border area within the republics or regions.

c) The families of those punished in accordance with the first category who live in Moscow, Leningrad, Kiev, Tbilisi, Baku, Rostov-on-the-Don, Taganrog, and in the districts of Sochi, Gagry, and Sukhumi, are subject to expulsion from these

---

the word "quotas" instead of "limits." Neither of these articles quotes the text of the order itself.

centers to other regions of their choice, except for districts near the border.

5. All families of persons punished in accordance with the first and second categories are to be registered and placed under systematic observation...

Investigation and carrying out of sentences:

IV. ORDER FOR CONDUCTING THE INVESTIGATION.

1. Investigation shall be conducted into the case of each person or group of persons arrested. The investigation shall be carried out in a swift and simplified manner. During the course of the trial, all criminal connections of persons arrested are to be disclosed.

2. At the conclusion of the investigation, the case is to be submitted for consideration to the troika. . . .

VI. ORDER OF IMPLEMENTATION OF SENTENCES.

1. The sentences are to be carried out by persons in accordance with instructions by the chairmen of the three-man commissions-i.e., by the people's commissars of the republic NKVDs, by the heads of governing boards, or by the regional departments of the NKVD. . . . The basis for the implementation of the sentence shall be the certified extract from the minutes of the troika session containing an account of the sentence regarding each convicted person and a special directive bearing the signature of the chairman of the troika, which are to be handed to the person who carries out the sentence.

2. The sentences included under the first category are to be carried out in places and in the order as instructed by the people's commissars of internal affairs, by the heads of governing boards, or by the

> regional departments of the NKVD. . . . Documents concerning the implementation of the sentence are attached in a separate envelope to the investigative dossier of each convicted person.
>
> 3. The assignment to camps of persons condemned under the second category is to be carried out on the basis of warrants communicated by the GULAG of the NKVD of the USSR.

During the Civil War and again during World War II the Bolsheviks declared martial law in areas close to the battlefront. Under martial law the rights citizens enjoyed under normal circumstances were sharply curtailed. Military commanders had ultimate authority over citizens and their property. Punishment of violations by citizens of military orders was harsh, and appeals were limited or not permitted at all.

Operational Order 00447 describes a situation that is *less* drastic than martial law. Citizens who did not fall into any of the categories set forth in Section I. 1-8 continued to live with their rights unimpaired. Normal legal and constitutional rights of citizens were only abrogated in the cases of persons caught in anti-Soviet acts. Only for them was normal judicial procedure abrogated.

Martial law would not have been appropriate because there were no armies, fronts, or battles. This was intended to be an operation against subversion by domestic enemies abetted by agents of hostile foreign countries – Germany, Japan, and Poland.

As in the case of martial law Order No. 00447 put a great deal of power into the hands of the authorized parties: the investigators and the police, the NKVD. The troika courts had power of summary execution or imprisonment of anyone against whom solid evidence was presented.

No. 00485 Polish Operation August 11, 1937

The "Polish Operation" of the NKVD was enabled by NKVD Order No. 00485 of August 11, 1937. It has been published many times in

Russian and is also online.[7] We have now made it available in English translation for the first time.[8]

The following are the major scholarly works on the Polish Operation.

* James Morris. "The Polish Terror: Spy Mania and Ethnic Cleansing in the Great Terror." *Europe-Asia Studies* 56, 5 (July 2004), 751-766.

* A. Ie. Gur'ianov, "Obzor sovetskikh repressivnykh kampanii protiv poliakov i pol'skikh grazhdan," in A. V. Lipatov and I. O. Shaitanov, eds., *Poliaki i russkie: Vzaimoponimanie i vzaimoneponimanie*, Moscow: Indrik, 2000, 199-207.

* A. Ie. Gur'ianov, "Obzor sovetskikh repressivnykh kampanii protiv poliakov i pol'skikh grazhdan," in *Massovye repressii protiv poliakov*. Memorial Society. At http://www.memo.ru/history/polacy/vved/index.htm This is a brief summary of Gur'ianov's longer article above.

* N. V. Petrov and A. B. Roginsksii, "'Pol'skaia operatsiia' NKVD 1937-1938 gg." in A. Ie. Gur'ianov, ed., *Repressii protiv poliakov i pol'skikh grazhdan*, Moscow: Zven'ia, 1997, 22-43. (Petrov & Roginskii)

All these studies agree in the following conclusions:

* The "Polish Operation" was aimed at Polish spies only, not at Poles as such. This can of course be seen from the text of Operational Order No. 00485 itself.

> The intention of the regime was not to terrorize or murder minority populations... (Morris 759)

> ... it [NKVD Order No. 00485, the "Polish Operation" order] did not concern Poles as such, but Polish spies... (Petrov & Roginskii)

---

[7] One site is http://ru.wikisource.org/wiki/Приказ_НКВД_от_11.08.1937_№_00485

[8] At http://msuweb.montclair.edu/~furrg/research/no00485.html

* Least of all was the massive nature of the repression "along Polish lines" the result of some kind of special personal hatred by Stalin of Poles. It was not a matter of Poles as such, but of Poland.

> ... their nationality was not a criterion of "criminal guilt" (prestupnosti) ...

> ...to equate the concept of "Poles" and "Polish operation" would be a mistake.(Petrov & Roginskii)

* Many of those arrested and either executed or imprisoned were not Poles or of Polish background at all. These numbers show that many of the victims were not ethnic Poles. (Morris 762)

* Petrov and Roginskii stress repeatedly that nationality itself was not a criterion for arrest or execution. The central NKVD did not keep records of the nationality of those arrested.

* In 1939, after his arrest for mass illegal repressions Ezhov confessed that he and his men had arrested people who were not Poles on the pretext that they were Poles:

> Uspensky, under the pretense of their being Poles, arrested many Ukrainian Uniates, that is, selected them not on the basis of national origin but according to their religion. I could multiply many times examples of this kind. They are characteristic for the majority of oblasts.

> (Ezhov interrogation of August 4, 1939)

We will discuss this more fully in the chapter on this confession of Ezhov's.

* There were few guidelines from Stalin and the Politburo — if, indeed, there were any at all. The whole operation was run by Ezhov and his men, who themselves gave little specific guidance to the local NKVD men. (Petrov & Roginskii)

Ezhov and his men got away with these immense crimes for many months. In his 1939 confessions Ezhov claimed that the Prosecutor's Office failed to conduct the oversight it was supposed to, and Ezhov and his men could shoot and imprison people with virtually no hindrance from Vyshinskii's office. This passage from Ezhov's interrogation of August 4, 1939, illustrates this negligence of Vy-shinskii's office:

> **Question**: Confess in what manner you managed to deceive the organs of prosecutorial oversight in implementing **this clear, obvious, and criminal practice of repression**?

> Answer: ...This inactivity of prosecutorial supervision can only be explained by the fact that **in charge of the Procuracy in many oblasts, krais, and republics were members of various anti-Soviet organizations who often practiced even more widespread provocational repressions among the population.**

This may account for the executions of Maslov and Mamonov, the prosecutors in Moscow when Khrushchev was First Secretary.

Ezhov continued:

> Another group of the prosecutors, those who were not involved in participation in anti-Soviet groupings, simply feared to argue with the heads of the UNKVDs on these questions, all the more so since they did not have any directives on these matters from the center...

> **Question:** You are talking about the local organs of the Procuracy. But didn't they see these criminal machinations in the Procuracy of the USSR?

> **Answer:** The Procuracy of the USSR could not, of course, have failed to notice all these perversions.

> I explain the behavior of the Procuracy of the USSR and, in particular, of Prosecutor of the USSR Vyshinskii by that same fear of quarreling with the NKVD and by [the desire] to prove themselves no less "revolutionary" in the sense of conducting mass repressions.

The first document issued after Ezhov had been induced to resign from office stressed the lack of Prosecutorial oversight.[9] On May 31, 1939 Vyshinskii was relieved of his post as Prosecutor of the USSR. It seems likely that this was because he had failed to do his duty during the *Ezhovshchina*.

No. 00486 – Wives and children August 15, 1937

This order called for the arrest and imprisonment of wives of those convicted of acts of treason since August 1 1936 – basically since the First Moscow Trial of later that month, the Zinoviev-Kamenev trial.

Certain wives were excluded from arrests: the pregnant; those with babies at the breast; the seriously or infectiously ill; those whose children were ill and needed care; those who were aged. Also, those who had given the authorities evidence against their husbands.

Children over the age of 15 who were considered "dangerous," capable of carrying out anti-Soviet acts, were subject to being sent to a labor camp. Others were to be put in orphanages. If the children wanted to remain with relatives or to work on their own and support themselves, this was to be permitted. Several sections of the Order give details about the treatment of and record-keeping concerning the children.

---

[9] "On Arrests, Supervision by the Procuracy, and the Conduct of Investigations." November 17, 1938. English translation at
https://msuweb.montclair.edu/~furrg/research/onarrestseng.html Also in Getty & Naumov, Document 190, 532-537.

Chapter 8. The Elections

Contested Elections to the Soviets Are Cancelled

The Central Committee Plenum of October 1937 saw the final cancellation of the plan for contested elections to the Soviets, the legislative branch of government. This represented a serious defeat for Stalin and his supporters in the Politburo. A sample ballot, showing several candidates, had already been drawn up. At least one copy of such a ballot has survived in an archive. Zhukov has included a photograph of it in Inoi, 6th illustration. I have put it online. [1]

Instead, the Soviet elections of December 1937 were implemented on the basis that the Party candidates would run on slates with 20-25% of non-party candidates – in other words, an "alliance" of sorts, but without a contest. Originally the elections were planned without slates; voting was to be only for individuals – a far more democratic method in that candidates would not get votes simply by being "on the ticket." (Zhukov, Zhupel 19 Nov. 02; Zhukov, Tainy. 41; Zhukov, Inoi 443)

Iakov Iakovlev

Iakov Iakovlev had been one of those closest to Stalin in drafting the 1936 Constitution to which Stalin was so committed. Along with A.I. Stetskii and B.M. Tal', Iakovlev was a member of the small commission that worked on the text of the constitution. They had presented a "rough draft" (*chernovoi nabrosok*) to Stalin in February 1936 – the draft that Stalin referred to in his celebrated talk with Roy Howard on March 1. (Zhukov, Inoi 223).

Evidently there had been some question on the part of some persons about trusting Iakovlev, who had been a Trotskyist in 1923. Stalin stood firmly by him. On April 3, 1937, Stalin had sent the

---

[1] At https://msuweb.montclair.edu/~furrg/research/sample_ballot_1937.html

following telegram to A.I. Krinitskii, secretary of the oblast' committee of the Party in Saratov:

> ... the CC of the VKP(b) considers that the obkom was incorrect to question the [political] reliability of com. Iakovlev, plenipotentiary of the Commission of Party Control. **The CC is aware of Com. Iakovlev's former waverings in 1922. These waverings were liquidated in 1924, and since that time com. Iakovlev has not given any occasion for any doubts whatever concerning his Bolshevik firmness. The CC trusts com. Iakovlev** and proposes that the obkom consider this matter close. (Zhukov, Inoi 370)

On June 27 Iakovlev delivered a report about the new electoral system to the June 1937 CC Plenum. After the Plenum Iakovlev continued to work on documents detailing how contested elections would be run. (Zhukov, Inoi 467) He met with Stalin several times in September and early October, no doubt to work on questions concerning the constitution. The electoral campaign for the contested Soviet elections was to begin on October 12.

But on October 10 all the members of the Politburo and Secretariat met in Stalin's office. The meeting ended at 10 p.m. after approving the main points of Molotov's presentation at the opening session of the CC Plenum, to be held the next day.

The second point of Molotov's presentation was:

> "Contested [literally "parallel"] candidates (not obligatory)."

Contested elections were effectively ruled out, since no one expected the regional Party leaders, the First Secretaries, to permit them unless they were required to do so. Moreover, point three of Molotov's outline reads: "Non-Party members: 20% - 25%."

What happened? Zhukov concludes that there was simply no majority in the Politburo, let alone the Central Committee, in support of contested elections and a strong insistence on guaranteeing that

the Party – which meant the regional Party leaders – would domi-
nate the Soviets.

Iakovlev's Arrest and Confession

On October 12, the day after the opening of the CC Plenum, Iakovlev was arrested. Two days later he confessed to having been a
clandestine Trotskyist "sleeper" since 1923. An even greater shock
was the fact that Iakovlev also confessed to having been recruited
by a German agent who told him that they, the Germans, were in
contact with Trotsky and wished to work with Iakovlev on the
same terms.

Iakovlev's confession is arguably one of the most important documents from the former Soviet archives published in recent years.
That no doubt explains why it is virtually never mentioned, let
alone studied, by mainstream historians of the USSR. Iakovlev inculpated as conspirators a number of leading Soviet figures.[2] In a
few cases we also have one or more confessions from some of
these figures which themselves confirm statements Iakovlev
makes here.

For example, Iakovlev names Rukhimovich as the person through
whom he contacted Piatakov. In the one interrogation of his that
has been published to date Rukhimovich details his conspiratorial
relationship with Piatakov. (Lubianka 1937-1938, No. 290)

For our purposes the significance of Iakovlev's confession is two-
fold.

First, he gives detailed testimony concerning the underground
conspiracy founded by Trotsky personally within the leading eche-
lons of the Bolshevik Party. Iakovlev told how he was recruited to
a secret Trotskyist conspiracy against the Party even before Lenin
had died. Iakovlev outlines his conspiratorial relations with,
among others, Piatakov and Ian Gamarnik. He had been especially
close to Gamarnik, from whom he learned directly about the mili-

---

[2] A full examination of the Iakovlev confession document is beyond the scope of this study.
We return to it in the second volume of our work on Trotsky.

tary conspiracy that included Marshal Tukhachevsky and Komandarms Iakir and Uborevich.

Second, Iakovlev outlines how he was recruited by German intelligence in 1935 in Berlin. The German agent who recruited him did so on two bases.

* From Russian émigrés in Germany the Germans knew that Iakovlev had collaborated with the Russian Tsarist Okhranka, or secret police, towards the end of 1916 in Petrograd. They blackmailed Iakovlev by threatening to expose this.

* The Germans knew about Iakovlev's participation in the Trotskyist underground from Trotsky himself.

> **Question**: You speak about GAMARNIK'S and VAREIKIS' connections with foreign intelligence services. Did you yourself have such connections?
>
> **Answer**: Yes, I had ties with German intelligence.
>
> **Question:** Tell us concretely, when did you establish ties with German intelligence?
>
> **Answer**: I was recruited by German intelligence when I was in Germany, in Berlin, in the autumn of 1935, and at that time and until my arrest I collaborated with this intelligence and maintained contact with it through a special representative in Moscow.
>
> In Berlin I was in the hospital "Catholic Commune" for treatment. About a week after my arrival in Berlin a man in a suit, whom I did not know, came to me in the hospital, and introduced himself to me by the name SHMUKE, and said that 'he had instructions to have discussions with me on a number of questions of interest to him and of urgency for me.' He announced that he knew 'from my political friends' about my membership in the underground organization that was struggling with the existing powers in the USSR and that, following

orders of the German government, he wished to establish businesslike relations with me....

Fearing a provocation, I naturally did not want to disclose myself to this unknown person and expressed my total confusion concerning what he had proposed to me. However, SHMUKE stubbornly continued that it was useless for me to deny facts that both he and I knew; that the German government was not turning to me alone, among leaders of underground organizations in the USSR, with such a proposal. **At last he said to me emphatically: "Your chief leader L. TROTSKY is acting in full contact and on the basis of mutual benefit with the new Germany."** I still attempted to end this conversation and made as though I wanted to stand up in order to say goodbye and force SHMUKE to leave. But SHMUKE did not budge from the spot and told me that I was too careful and, clearly, did not trust him; that this carefulness was a good sign in me, on the one hand, however, he had the full possibility of proving to me the 'official nature' of his visit and had the full information of the German government about me.... Then he said that "in Germany live emigrants from Russia, including former members of the Russian police, who have informed the German authorities about certain episodes of my collaboration with the Russian police at the end of 1916 in Petrograd. Although they had the full ability to compromise me with the Soviet authorities at any moment they, said SHMUKE, did not wish to do that, since **they hope to establish with me the same kind of contact as they have with TROTSKY."**

I understood that I had fallen into a pitfall and there was no other way out. Faced with this fact, and realizing that the Germans were fully informed about me, I decided to agree with SHMUKE'S proposal, all the more since **SHMUKE'S information about TROTSKY'S connections with Germany completely corresponded with what PIATAKOV had said to me and what TROTSKY had written.**

... Considering the matter more thoroughly, I decided that if possible I would sell my collaboration to the Germans more dearly, first of all to obtain from German intelligence corresponding possibilities for foreign connections for our organization and, in the first place, with TROTSKY, and also to increase my importance in the eyes of the German government.

(Lubianka 1937-1938, 394-5)

Iakovlev admits direct ties with German intelligence. This confirms allegations by others that Trotsky's movement had such contacts. He also confirms German ties of Gamarnik – that is, the Military conspirators led by Tukhachevsky – and Vareikis, head of the Party in the Far East.

There is no reason to think that Iakovlev had been forced to make a false confession. He had worked closely with Stalin for a long time. As we have seen, Stalin had stood up for him when the oblast committee of the Saratov Party had questioned Iakovlev's political reliability. But the oblast committee had been right -- Stalin had been wrong. Iakovlev had worked so closely with Stalin that it is very likely Stalin met with him to ask whether his confession was truthful. We know that he did this in other cases – with Piatakov and Bukharin, for example.

We do know that Stalin believed that Iakovlev's confession was truthful. The following document in this same volume is a copy of Stalin's handwritten questions.

1) Did he know about Vareikis' service with the Tsarist secret police (okhranke)?

> 2) His opinion about Mikhailov from Voronezh and his participation in the c.-r. org. [counter-revolutionary organization – GF].

> 3) His contact with Trotsky (did he see him personally in 1935 or in 1934).

> 4) How did he want to use MOPR? Whom in MOPR did he make use of? [*Mezhdunarodne Obshchestvo Pomoshchi Revoliutsioneram*, International Organization for Aid to Revolutionaries, the Soviets' organization to give help to revolutionaries in fascist countries where communist parties were illegal and subject to severe repression. – GF]

> 5) "Turn" Iakovlev's wife: he is a conspirator and she must tell us everything. Ask her about Stasova, Kirsanova, and other friends – acquaintances of hers. (Lubianka 1937-1938, No. 227 396)

Stalin also voiced the same suspicions about Elena Stasova and Klavdiia Kirsanova to Georgii Dimitrov. But neither Stasova nor Kirsanova was even arrested, much less convicted or punished.

Therefore Stalin was trying to find out the truth. This is important because it means that a serious investigation about Iakovlev took place. It also provides additional evidence for the existence of a widespread Trotsky-German conspiracy that included high officials in Soviet society.

Party and Trade Union Elections

Contested elections were not held for the Soviets (councils). But they were held for Party and trade union positions. At the February-March 1937 CC Plenum

> Zhdanov called for the 'democratization' of party organizations in the regions. This meant secret ballot re-election of all party organs from top to bottom, periodic reporting of party organs to their organizations, strict party discipline, and subordination of the minority to the majority, and

> unconditional obligatory decisions of higher bodies
> on all party members. He complained about co-
> option (appointment) to party buros rather than
> election, and candidates for leading positions being
> considered behind closed doors, 'in family order'.
> ...This was a virtual declaration of war against the
> regional clan leaderships, and their reaction in the
> discussion to Zhdanov's report (which they at first
> unprecedentedly greeted with angry silence)
> showed that they were angry. (Getty, Rise 77)

Stalin and the central Party leadership pushed hard for Party elections.

> Based on a strong keynote speech by A. A. Zhdanov,
> seconded by Stalin, the plenum had attacked the
> high-handed, authoritarian, and "undemocratic"
> practices that had made regional party secretaries
> such powerful magnates. Making a play for
> grassroots support against the "feudal princes," the
> Central Committee denounced the secretaries for a
> lack of self-criticism and scheduled new party
> elections for the spring of 1937. The election
> proposal showed that Stalin and his leadership
> were becoming serious about trying to weaken the
> power of the territorial secretaries. **The voting was
> to be by secret ballot, with multiple candidates
> nominated from below** and was therefore a direct
> assault on the regional party barons' patronage
> power. Both Zhdanov and Stalin called for much
> stronger criticism and self-criticism by the party
> bosses. (Getty, Practicing 203)

During the months following the February-March CC Plenum the
Party elections described by Zhdanov were actually held.

> The elections were in fact so conducted. See
> Smolensk Archive, files WKP 110, pp. 258–79; WKP
> 322, pp. 52–57; WKP 105,

passim. For the national election results, see
Pravda, 23 May 1937. Nationally, about half of all
party secretaries were voted out of office. (Getty,
Practicing 334 n. 79)

The Party elections gave rise to excitement among the rank-and-file.

The center was stimulating criticism of local leaders
on the eve of the elections. "Little people" were
being encouraged to speak up. As unofficial
accounts and novels of the time show, there were
already many of the rank and file complaining
about local leaders even before 1937. Both the
novelist Kataev and the American worker John
Scott described an atmosphere in which there was
always grassroots, enthusiast discontent with local
leaders. The Smolensk Archive contains many files
of complaint letters from average citizens about the
abuses of lower and higher officials. These letters
were sent to newspapers, prosecutors, and party
officials and reflect widespread and often bitter
discontent on lower levels. **The February plenum
awakened and unleashed this sentiment; it did
not create it. The meetings after the plenum saw
for the first time a situation in which rank-and-
file members stood up at meetings and openly
disagreed with reports they had just heard.**
(Getty, Origins 161)

It appears that it was mainly lower-level Party officials who failed
in re-election and were replaced by new people.

... it seems clear that the main attrition in the
secretarial ranks occurred below raion level. Of the
dozens of raikom first secretaries across the region,
only nine failed reelection. Raion party committees
were turned over by half, and most of the
replacement was at this level or below.

> More than half of the lower-level party leadership
> was turned out of office in secret-ballot voting that
> took place after open (and sometimes insulting)
> criticism from the floor.... (Getty, Origins 161-162)

A more recent article shows this result in one area, Iaroslavl'.

> Over the next few weeks, the Iaroslavl' party
> organization held the new party elections by secret
> ballot mandated by Zhdanov in his speech to the
> February plenum... In 726 of 1,272 (57 per cent)
> primary party organizations of the oblast', the
> election meetings had found party work
> 'unsatisfactory', and in Iaroslavl' it was higher (67
> per cent). Across the oblast', there were objections
> to 26 per cent of the proffered candidates (32 per
> cent in Iaroslavl'). Nevertheless, the Vainov clan
> retained its hold on top positions. Although 36 per
> cent of the new party secretaries in major party
> organizations were new cadres elected for the first
> time, 'in the large party organizations, the old cadre
> partkom secretaries were preserved'. (Getty, Rise
> 81)

Getty believes that Stalin and Zhdanov really wanted to break up
local cliques but failed, perhaps inevitably.

> Given the ability of the local leaders to control and
> influence events, it might seem naive of Stalin and
> Zhdanov to hope that the local machines would
> reform themselves. But what choices did they have?
> Their past attempts to secure "fulfillment of
> decisions" had included public exhortations by
> Stalin, control-commission inspectors, and strong
> press denunciations of particular offenders. When
> these failed, Stalin and Zhdanov proposed
> reeducation of the secretaries, attempted to strip
> the secretaries of their patronage power, and tried
> to achieve control from below with new elections.
> Populist control from below was not naive; rather,

**it was a vain but sincere attempt to use the rank
and file to break open the closed regional
machines. (**Getty, Origins 162)

Stalin did indeed have democratic intentions. Relying on the rank-
and-file to vote out local leaders, if they chose to do so, is one of
the things democracy is all about.

At the same February-March 1937 CC Plenum Shvernik had called
for contested Trade Union elections:

> Shvernik argued that the unions, like the Party,
> lacked internal democracy.
>
> "1 should say here, directly and with all frankness,"
> he explained, "that the unions are in even worse
> shape." With the development of new industries
> during the first five-year plan, the country's 47
> unions had split into 165, creating thousands of
> new jobs. Positions at every level were filled by
> appointment, rather than election....Shvernik
> concluded his speech with the suggestion that
> elections were needed not only in the Party, but in
> the unions as well. ... "1 think this would clean our
> ranks of bureaucratic elements, closely connect us
> with the broad masses, and give the unions the
> chance to get closer to the masses." (Goldman,
> Terror 126.)

In April and May 1937 the Sixth Plenum of the All-Union Council of
Trade Unions had called for new, secret ballot elections to union
positions.

> The resolutions adopted by the 6th Plenum
> demanded that the unions be recast, from top to
> bottom. New elections based on secret ballots were
> to be held in every union organization from central
> to factory committees. Union members would have
> "the unlimited right to reject and criticize"
> individual candidates. Voting by lists was
> forbidden. The plenum mandated deadlines as well:

> elections for factory and shop committees were to
> be held between June l and July 15, followed by
> regional (oblast) conferences, union congresses,
> and elections for higher-level posts between July 15
> and September 15. (Goldman, Terror 141)

During the second half of 1937 the unprecedented democratic
trade union elections were in fact conducted.

> By the end of 1937, new central committees were
> elected in 146 of the country's l57 unions. Party and
> union leaders proclaimed the campaign a great
> success. About 1,230,000 people or 6 percent of the
> 22 million membership were elected to union posts,
> including 31,000 to regional (oblast' and krai) and
> republic committees, 830,000 to factory
> committees, 160,000 to shop committees, and
> 163,000 to group organizations (profgrupy**). The
> VTsSPS nullified hundreds of elections that
> violated "the principles of union democracy" by
> not offering secret ballots and more than one
> candidate. This "made a deep impression on the
> workers," according to one report.** (Goldman,
> Terror 147)

> Party and VTsSPS leaders pointed with pride to the
> fact that many newly elected officials were not
> party members, evidence that "new people," "the
> best Stakhanovites," were becoming active in union
> affairs... **Party leaders' active endorsement of
> nonparty candidates stood in sharp contrast to
> their usual policy of promoting their own
> members.** (Goldman, Terror 148-149)

But in 1939, after the abandonment of secret, contested elections
for the legislative bodies (soviets), such elections were abandoned
in the trade unions as well.

> In spring 1939, union and party leaders stealthily
> reversed the campaign for union democracy. The
> Moscow party committee called a joint meeting of

heads of the partkomy and factory committees. Shvernik, the head of the VTsSPS, explained that the Moscow party committee would "oversee" the upcoming union elections. **New rules abolished direct elections.**

... [O]fficials were instructed to disguise the fact that voting by list, a practice banned in 1937, was reinstituted. The campaign for union democracy had been linked at its inception to democratic national elections to the Supreme Soviet. The ill-fated experiments in democracy were also twinned in their demise. Shvernik noted that Moscow party officials had decided to abolish direct union elections based on their experience with elections to the Supreme Soviet. *Profdemokratiia* - union democracy- the great rallying cry of 1937, was dead. (Goldman, Terror 258-259)

The forces that were powerful enough to defeat Stalin's struggle for democratic, contested elections to the legislative branch of the Soviet government, the soviets, had not been powerful enough to stop democratic elections in the Party and the Trade Unions. These did take place in 1937. But they did not happen again.

Chapter 9. The Mass Repressions Are Stopped

Accounts of the repressions of 1937-1938 by mainstream historians are useful insofar as they document how the repressions proceeded. By surveying the large number of primary sources now available the mainstream accounts show how Stalin and the top Party leadership gradually came to understand what was happening. What they had been told was a battle against counterrevolutionary conspiracies had in fact very often been directed against loyal Party members and completely innocent citizens.

But mainstream historians do not discuss the most important sets of documentary evidence that bear directly on the causes, course, and conclusion of the Ezhov mass repressions:

* The conspiracies that we know existed. This includes all those that were the subject of the three Moscow Trials plus the conspiracy of military commanders and other officers that is often referred to simply as the Tukhachevsky Affair. These conspiracies provided the impetus for the resolutions of early June 1937 concerning the need to use massive force.

* The investigation documents detailing the confessions of alleged conspirators and the conclusions of NKVD investigators with which Ezhov bombarded Stalin and the central Party leadership for more than a year after the June 1937 CC Plenum. Dozens of these reports, often very long and always very detailed, have been published. We cited the principal document collections in a previous chapter. Only a few have been translated into English. Iakov Iakovlev's confession is one of them. We don't know how much more documentation Stalin received. This is probably just a fraction of it.

* The confession of Ezhov's assistant Mikhail Frinovskii of April 1939 and Ezhov's many confessions of 1939 are entirely ignored by mainstream scholars.

The few remarks mainstream historians make about this material shows that they prefer to "not believe" it. This is the fallacy of "begging the question," "assuming that which is to be proven." It is illegitimate for historians to ignore evidence simply because that evidence is not consistent with some preconceived paradigm of "what must have happened." But these confessions dismantle the "anti-Stalin paradigm." Consequently, they are ignored.

Mainstream scholarship ignores all the evidence that explains the reason for the mass repression of the Ezhov era. Then these scholars declare that the reason for these repressions is a mystery: "We will never know" why they took place, and so on. Naturally, if one decides in advance to ignore the evidence, then the events are indeed "inexplicable."

* * * * *

Already at the October 1937 CC Plenum the first protest against the mass repressions was uttered by Kursk First Secretary Peskarov:

> They [the NKVD? The troika? – GF] condemned
> people for petty stuff... illegally, and when we ... put
> the question to the C.C., comrades Stalin and
> Molotov strongly supported us and sent a brigade
> of workers from the Supreme Court and
> Prosecutor's office to review these cases ... And it
> turned out that for three weeks' work of this
> brigade 56% of the sentences in 16 *raiony* were set
> aside by the brigade as illegal. What's more, in 45%
> of the sentences there was no evidence that a crime
> had been committed. (Zhukov, Tainy, 43)

Getty cites some signs that Ezhov's activities may have come under some negative scrutiny as early as December 1937. (Origins 182-185) He concludes:

> **The police had been implicitly insulted and
> criticized in late 1937,** particularly when they

tried to associate themselves with rank-and-file interests. Yet Ezhov's NKVD establishment remained strong despite transfers and Ezhov's simultaneous duties at Water Transport. **Stalin wanted to stop local chaos without totally discrediting the NKVD,** for he supported continued investigations and repression of oppositionists and other "suspicious" persons. (Getty Origins 188)

The January 1938 CC Plenum

It appears that this Plenum was called in a hurry to deal with a serious situation of mass expulsions and arrests of Party members, including many Party officials.

> Sometime around the beginning of the year, Politburo member A. A. Andreev was assigned the task of gathering compromising material on Postyshev's party expulsions in Kuibyshev. These documents included **documentation of mass party expulsions** from the Kuibyshev soviet, from the ranks of party district committee secretaries, and from other organizations. One report from the Bazarno-Syzgansky district noted that **large numbers had been expelled as enemies by order of Postyshev's men, though the NKVD subsequently found reason to arrest very few of them.**

> ... based on the materials Andreev compiled, the Politburo decided only on 7 January to use the occasion of a Supreme Soviet meeting to convene a plenum for 11 January, a lead time of only four days. (Getty & Naumov 498-499; 501)

Pavel Postyshev, First Secretary of the Kuibyshev oblast' committee of the Party, was sharply criticized and then removed first from his position as Candidate Member of the Politburo and then, at the end of the month, from his position as First Secretary of the Kuibyshev obkom.

Postyshev's actions had shocked Stalin and other Politburo members.

> Beria: Is it possible that all members of the plenums
> of the raion committees were enemies?

> Kaganovich: There is no basis to say that they are
> all swindlers.

> Stalin evaluated Postyshev's methods this way:
> "This is the massacre of the organization. They are
> very easy on themselves, but they're shooting
> everybody in the raion organizations.... This means
> stirring up the party masses against the CC, it can't
> be understood any other way."[1]

Postyshev later admitted to being a member of the Right-Trotskyist conspiracy and deliberately wrecking the Party apparatus.

Molotov told Vladimir Karpov that he had doubted that Postyshev was guilty. Stalin suggested that he, Molotov, and Marshal Voroshilov go to interview Postyshev personally. Karpov writes:

> In my conversations with Molotov at his dacha we
> had a conversation about the repressions. Once I
> asked:

> – Is it possible that you never had any doubts? After
> all, they were arresting people whom you knew
> well by their work even before the revolution, and
> then also in the Civil War.

> – Doubts did arise, once I spoke to Stalin about this,
> and he answered: "Go to the Lubianka and check on
> this yourself, take Voroshilov here with you.

---

[1] *Stalinskoe Politbiuro v 30-e gody*, pp. 161-4. See the Russian text of this session with Postyshev from *Stalinskoe Politbiuro...* at
http://msuweb.montclair.edu/~furrg/research/postyshev0138.pdf

Voroshilov was then in the office. We both went right away. Those were exactly the days when we had fresh doubts about the arrest of Postyshev. We drove to Ezhov. He ordered Postyshev's file to be brought out. We looked through the transcripts of interrogations. Postyshev admitted his guilt. I said to Ezhov: "I want to have a talk with Postyshev himself." He was brought. He was pale, had lost weight, and generally looked depressed. **I asked him: Were his confessions written down accurately in the transcripts of interrogation? He answered: They are written correctly. I asked again – "That means, you admit that you are guilty?" He was silent, and somehow reluctantly answered: "Since I signed them, that means, I admit it, what is there to say..." That's how it was. How could we not believe it, when the man himself said it?"**[2]

The Politburo sent Andrei A. Andreev to Kuibyshev to make an on-the-spot checkup. Below are parts of the letter Andreev sent to Stalin on January 31, 1938, about Postyshev's lawless and arbitrary repressions:

2) Since August about 3,000 members have been expelled from the party, a significant part of whom were expelled without any basis whatsoever as "enemies of the people" or their confederates. At the plenum of the oblast committee the secretaries of the raion committees brought forward facts, when Postyshev became arbitrary and demanded the expulsion and arrest of honest party members either for the slightest criticism at party meetings of the leadership of the oblast committee [i.e. Postyshev himself] or even without any basis at all.

---

[2] Karpov, Vladimir Vasil'evich. *Marshal Zhukov, ego soratnikii i protivniki v gody voiny i mira.* *Book* 1. Chapter 6, "The Tukhachevsky Affair." http://militera.lib.ru/bio/karpov/06.html

In general this whole tone came from the oblast committee.

3) Since all these matters look like a provocation, we had to arrest a few of the most suspicious, zealous deviationists from the oblast and city committees, the former second secretary Filimonov, the obcom workers Sirotinskii, Alakin, Fomenko, and others. **At the very first interrogations they all confessed that they were members of a Right-Trotskyite organization up to the present. Surrounding Postyshev and enjoying his full confidence, they developed their disorganizational and provocational work of dissolving the party organizations and mass expulsions of party members.** We also had to arrest Pashkovskii, Postyshev's assistant. **He confessed that he had concealed the fact that he had been a Social-Revolutionary in the past, had been recruited to the Right-Trotskyite organization in 1933 in Kiev, and obviously was a Polish spy. He was one of the most active of those in Postyshev's circle in the matter of arbitrariness and disorganization in Kuybyshev.** We are untangling matters further, in order to unmask this gang.[3]

A resolution of the January 1938 Plenum hinted that those who use "formalistic and callously bureaucratic attitude" towards Party members might really be "cleverly disguised enemies who try to disguise their hostility with shouts about vigilance, in that way to maintain themselves in the Party ranks, who strive through repressive measures to beat up our Bolshevik cadres and to sow uncertainty and excess suspicion in our ranks."

---

[3] *Sovetskoe rukovodstvo. Perepiska. 1928-1941*. ed. A.V. Kvashonkin et al., Moscow: ROSSPEN, 1999, p. 387. Full text at
http://msuweb.montclair.edu/~furrg/research/andreevrepostyshev0138.pdf

> During the January 1938 Plenum, more leaders
> criticized excesses in the examination of personal
> cases of communists. Politburo candidate member
> Zhdanov demanded that people should not be
> accused without grounds and that accusations
> against every suspect should be investigated.
> Kalinin wanted people to be judged on the basis of
> their actions instead of their relations. Even
> Molotov thought that people who had erred should
> be distinguished from wreckers. (Jansen & Petrov
> 125-6)

Postyshev himself was arrested on February 22, 1938. On April 9 he wrote a statement to Ezhov in which he said he would "give the investigation a frank confession about his counterrevolutionary activity against the Party and Soviet power, which I have been carrying out for a number of years." The investigation determined that "P.P. Postyshev, for a number of years, had been a member of the center of the Right-Trotskyist organization in the Ukraine. In his subversive work he was connected with Kosior, Chubar', Balit-skii, Iakir, Ashrafian, Veger, Kosarev, and others." He was accused of having been a Japanese spy since 1920.

Postyshev confessed against others and reiterated his confession at trial. (Furr, Khrushchev No. 23, text and Appendix). His trial was in February, 1939, after Beria had replaced Ezhov as commissar of the NKVD and had begun to re-investigate all those repressed under Ezhov.

We have a little documentation about early suspicion by the Polit-buro against the NKVD itself.

> In early 1938, the Central Committee sent
> Shkiriatov to Ordzhonikidze to "investigate
> evidence that had come through about criminal
> perversions during the mass operations"
> committed by regional NKVD organs. Jansen &
> Petrov 135)

According to Iurii Zhukov, Stalin warned Ezhov twice. The first time was in April 1938, when Ezhov was named to be Commissar for Water Transportation. Getty states:

> ... it could not have escaped notice that Yezhov's predecessor Yagoda had been eased out of his police position by first appointing him to a similar post. (Getty & Naumov 528)

The second warning was unmistakable. On August 22 Beria replaced Frinovskii as Ezhov's assistant.

Genrikh Liushkov Defects to the Japanese June 1938

On June 13, 1938, NKVD General Genrikh S. Liushkov walked across the border between Soviet Siberia and Japanese-occupied Manchuria and defected. Within a few days he had given press conferences during which he attacked Stalin and denounced all the Moscow Trials and the Tukhachevsky Affair as fabrications. To his Japanese military handlers, however, Liushkov admitted that the conspiracies were genuine.

> Later, Frinovskii testified that during the summer of 1937 the Georgian NKVD had sent them T. I. Lordkipanidze's testimony that Liushkov belonged to the "conspirators around Iagoda," but Ezhov had not only withheld the evidence from the Central Committee but had also appointed Liushkov Far Eastern NKVD chief. He had instructed Frinovskii to reinterrogate Iagoda, thereby leaving Liushkov out of it. Understanding what was expected of him, Iagoda had testified that Liushkov was not involved in the conspiracy.
>
> ... Testimony by L. G. Mironov and others about Liushkov's conspiratorial activities was also withheld. ... In March or April, when reinterrogating Mironov, Ezhov induced him to retract his testimony against Liushkov. Around the same time, on 16 April, Liushkov's deputy, M. A. Kagan, was

> summoned to Moscow and arrested upon arrival.
> According to Frinovskii, this was meant to signal
> Liushkov to commit suicide, but he did not react.
> The Central Committee wanted him dismissed soon.
> A second signal was Ezhov's telegram to Liushkov
> of late May 1938 about his promotion to the central
> NKVD apparatus in Moscow. But Liushkov, instead
> of committing suicide, escaped to Japan. (Jansen &
> Petrov 144-145)

This evidence that Liushkov was involved with Ezhov in a real conspiracy – a fact we also know from the other sources mentioned above – contradicts Jansen and Petrov's position that no such conspiracies existed.

August 22 1938: Beria replaces Frinovskii

On August 22, 1938 Lavrentii Beria was appointed Assistant Commissar of the NKVD, replacing Mikhail Frinovskii. According to the evidence now available Ezhov considered this to be a hostile move against himself.

> Significantly, by 10 August there were rumors that
> a new deputy was to be appointed to Ezhov and
> that this boded ill for him. It was no accident that
> the largest group of prisoners was shot in a rush on
> 29 July; a month later, on 26 and 29 August,
> another group was shot, including Zakovskii, Salyn',
> and L. G. Mironov . Ezhov was in a hurry to get rid
> of people who might testify against him.
>
> On 22 August 1938, the Georgian Party leader,
> Lavrentii Beria, was made First Deputy People's
> Commissar of the Interior. Ezhov, it appears, had
> started collecting incriminating evidence against
> him, in connection with his growing influence.
> (Jansen & Petrov 148)
>
> On 27–28 August Frinovskii met with Evdokimov,
> who insisted that before Beria arrived he must take
> care of any unfinished cases (*nedodelki*) that might

compromise them. He told Frinovskii: "Check to see
whether Zakovskii and all Iagoda people have been
executed, because after Beria's arrival the
investigation of these cases may be renewed and
they may turn against us." Frinovskii then
ascertained that a group of Chekists, including
Zakovskii and Mironov, had been shot on 26–27
August (actually they were shot on 29 August).
**Ezhov, Frinovskii, and Evdokimov were with
good reason concerned about Chekists who had
been arrested on charges of conspiracy and
might under Beria's regime testify against
Ezhov's circle, or even against Ezhov himself. It
was no accident that the executions took place
in a hurry in late August, while Beria was away
in Georgia. (**Jansen & Petrov 151)

Here as elsewhere, Jansen and Petrov's text is compatible only
with the hypothesis which these same authors reject: that Ezhov
himself was involved in a conspiracy against the Soviet government.

A Politburo resolution of 8 October formed a special
commission to study arrest procedures and the
apparent lack of judicial supervision over police
activities. (Getty & Naumov 529.)

Although Ezhov chaired the special commission, Beria was on it
and none of Ezhov's NKVD men were members.

November 1938: Orders to stop all mass repressions.

On November 15 1938 the hearing of cases by troikas were
stopped, along with military tribunals and the Military Collegium
of the Supreme Court.

15 November 1938

> To confirm the following directives by the Council
> of People's Commissars
>
> (SNK) of the USSR and of the CC of the VKP(b) . . .
>
> It is ordered in the most strict terms:
>
> 1. To stop from November 16 of this year until
> further notice the review of all cases by troikas,
> military tribunals, and the Military Collegium of the
> Supreme Court of the USSR, that have been sent for
> their review by special orders or by any other
> simplified procedure.
>
> ...
>
> V. Molotov, Chairman of the Council of People's
> Commissars (SNK)
>
> I. Stalin, Secretary of the CC of the VKP(b)
> (Lubianka 1937-1938 606 No. 361; Getty &
> Naumov 531-2.

On November 17, 1938 was issued the Decree of the Central Committee "On arrests, prosecutorial supervision, and conduct of investigations."[4] An important section of this decree reads as follows:

> ... [E]nemies of the people and spies employed by
> foreign intelligence agencies, having wormed their
> way into both the central and local organs of the
> NKVD and continuing their subversive activities,
> sought in every way possible to hamper the work of
> investigators and agents. They sought to
> consciously pervert Soviet laws by carrying out
> mass, unjustified arrests while at the same time
> rescuing their confederates (especially those who
> had joined the NKVD) from destruction.

---

[4] Shearer, Lubianka 221-4; Getty & Naumov, 532-7). Online at
http://istmat.info/node/36068 and many other sites; Lubianka 1937-1938 No. 362, 607-611. English translation online at
https://msuweb.montclair.edu/~furrg/research/onarrestseng.html

The chief deficiencies, brought to light recently, in the work of the NKVD and the Procuracy are as follows:

First of all, **officials of the NKVD had totally abandoned the work with agents and informers in favor of the much simpler method of making mass arrests without concerning themselves with the completeness or with the high quality of the investigation.**

November 22, 1938: Ezhov resigns

Iurii Zhukov says that he has held in his hand the resignation statement Ezhov signed on November 23, 1938.

> On November 23 Ezhov was again summoned to Stalin's office. Molotov and Voroshilov were already present. I have held in my hands the document that Ezhov signed, evidently at their dictation. It is written on three pages, all of different dimension. That is they grabbed the first sheets of paper they could get their hands on and passed them to Ezhov just so that he would not stop writing. The formula of his leaving his position is changed twice. Evidently he protested, offered some resistance. But it was necessary to wrest from him a decision to resign "according to his own desire." ... The Politburo sent around telegrams with the direct instructions: Immediately stop repressions and dissolve the "troikas." Having seized the initiative, the Stalin group once again at the end of 1938 managed to conduct the first trials at law of NKVD workers accused of the falsification and fabrication of cases. Through these trials, over a period of almost a year, were tried and exiled or executed thousands of persons. This is how the great terror was brought to an end. (Zhukov, *Komsomolskaia Pravda* 20 Nov. 2002.)

Getty notes that the process of review and rehabilitation of Ezhov's victims began immediately.

> On December 8, the press announced that he had been relieved of his duties as head of the NKVD "at his own request." Four days later, the Moscow Regional Court reversed the first of many convictions of former "enemies." **The declaration noted that the Supreme Court had not only released five construction engineers but had recognized that the five had actually tried to thwart "real enemies."** (Getty, Origins 188-189)

Chapter 10. The Ezhov Conspiracy

Ezhov's Conspiracy Gradually Uncovered

> "...legality is reintroduced under Beriya, November 1938." (Wheatcroft, Agency 41)

By the time of the October 1937 CC Plenum Stalin and the Politburo had begun to uncover evidence of massive illegal repressions. Suspicions continued to grow in the Politburo that massive, unauthorized repressions were going on. In August 1938 Ezhov's second-in-command, Mikhail Frinovskii, was replaced by Lavrentii Beria. Beria was chosen as a reliable person to keep watch over Ezhov, as Ezhov himself later stated.

As soon as Ezhov resigned, to be replaced by Beria, orders were given to immediately stop all the repressions, to repeal all the NKVD Operational Orders that enabled them, to stop the work of the troikas and to re-emphasize the need for oversight by the Prosecutor's Office of all cases of arrest.[1]

After this there began a flood of reports to Beria and the central Party leadership concerning massive illegitimate repressions and shootings on the part of local NKVD groups. We have many of these documents now, and no doubt there are many more of them. The central Party leadership began to investigate.

On January 29, 1939 Beria, Andreev, and Malenkov signed a report about the massive abuses during Ezhov's tenure. (Petrov & Iansen 359-363) [2] This very important evidence that the massive repression was Ezhov's, not Stalin's, doing was only published in 2008. It begins as follows:

---

[1] This document is available in English in Getty & Naumov Doc. 190 pp. 532-537.

[2] Russian text online at http://istmat.info/node/24582 English translation at http://msuweb.montclair.edu/~furrg/research/beria_andreev_malenkov012939eng.html

We consider it essential to report to you the following conclusions about the situation of cases in the NKVD USSR:

1. **During the period of time that com. Ezhov headed the Narkomvnudel** [People's Commissariat of Internal Affairs, the NKVD] of the USSR right up until the moment he left the duties of People's Commissar **a majority of the leading positions in the NKVD USSR and in the organs under its supervision (the NKVDs of union and autonomous republics, the UNKVDs of the krais and oblasts) have been occupied by enemies of the people, conspirators, and spies.**

2. Enemies of the people who penetrated the organs of the NKVD have consciously distorted the punitive policy of Soviet power, have carried out **massive, unfounded arrests of completely innocent persons, while at the same time covering up real enemies of the people.**

3. The methods of conducting investigations have been perverted in the most brutal manner. **They had recourse to beatings of prisoners on a massive level in order to force them into false confessions and "admissions."** The quantity of admissions that each investigator was supposed to obtain from prisoners in the course of 24 hours has been decided upon in advance. In addition, the quotas have often reached several dozen "admissions."

Investigators have widely made use of the practice of fully informing one another concerning the content of the confessions they obtained. This gave the investigators the ability, during interrogations of "their" prisoners, to suggest to them by one means or another facts, circumstances, and names of persons about whom confessions had earlier been given by other prisoners. As a result this kind of investigation very often led to **organized false slanders against persons who were completely innocent.**

In order to obtain a greater number of admissions a number of organs of the NKVD had recourse to direct provocation: **they convinced prisoners to give confessions about supposed espionage work for foreign intelligence services by explaining that these kinds of fabricated confessions were needed by the party and government in order to discredit foreign states.** They also promised the prisoners that they would be liberated after they gave such "admissions."

The leadership of the NKVD in the person of com. Ezhov not only did not put a stop to this kind of arbitrariness and extremism in arrests and in the conduct of investigations, but sometimes itself abetted it.

The slightest attempts by Chekist party members to oppose this arbitrariness were stifled.

[...]

Com. Ezhov concealed in every way from the Central Committee of the ACP(b) the situation of the work in the NKVD organs. Besides that he hid from the CC ACP(b) materials that compromised leading NKVD workers.

...]

In addition we believe it essential to note that **all the above disgraceful actions, distortions and excesses <in the matter of arrests and the conduct of investigation> were carried out with the sanction and knowledge of the organs of the Procuracy of the USSR (coms. Vyshinskii and**

Roginsky). Assistant Procuror of the USSR
Roginsky has been especially zealous in this matter.
Roginsky's practice of work raises serious doubts
about his political honesty <and reliability>.[3]

The report continues in this vein.

Reports and investigations of NKVD abuses continued rapidly. In
April Mikhail Frinovskii, Ezhov's former deputy commissar, and
Ezhov himself were arrested. They immediately began to confess.

We have put online all of Ezhov's confessions published so far in
both the Russian original and in English translation.[4] These confessions revealed the broad outlines of Ezhov's conspiracy against
and deception of the Soviet leadership and of Stalin. We will examine them in the next four chapters.

During the next few years, until to the beginning of the war and
even beyond, further investigations and prosecutions of guilty
NKVD men proceeded. According to the editors of a major document collection:

> **...in 1939 the NKVD arrested more than 44
> thousand persons, about one-fifteenth of the
> number arrested in 1938.** Most of these arrests
> were in Western Ukraine and Belorussia [as a result
> of the retaking of these territories from Poland in
> September 1939 and the arrests of Polish officials
> and settlers – GF]. **During the same year about
> 110,000 persons were freed after the review of
> cases of those arrested in 1937-1938.** (Lubianka
> 1939-1946, 564 n. 11)

"Memorial" society researchers Okhotin and Roginskii agree:

> The investigation of cases of arrested persons
> continued after November 17, 1938 in a
> significantly gentler manner. **This was due ... to**

---

[3] According to the editors, the text within angled brackets is handwritten in the original.

[4] See "Additional Bibliography — Documents" at the bottom of the following page:
http://msuweb.montclair.edu/~furrg/research/trials_Ezhovshchina_update0710.html

the renewal of prosecutorial supervision. On
November 27 Vyshinskii ordered the prosecutors
on all levels to make the strict supervision of the
NKVD of the proper procedures their primary duty
and to report all violations to the Chief Procuracy of
the USSR. ... **Along with the investigation of
unfinished cases also went the review of
sentences already handed down. ... [A]ccording
to our present information, during the year
1939 around 100,000 persons who had earlier
been convicted of counterrevolutionary crimes
were freed. (**TSD 5, 2 517)

Michael Ellman, a scholar very hostile to Stalin, refers to the "reports of hundreds of thousands of sentences being overturned."
Determined to say something negative Ellman continues:

On the other hand there are complaints about the
unwillingness of the organs to disgorge prisoners
and the slowness of the re-examination process.
(Ellman, Trials 1317 n.20)

A great many cases were reviewed and at least 110,000 prisoners
freed. But the engine of repression was slow to turn around. On
May 31, 1939 Vyshinskii sent Stalin and Molotov another note
suggesting that more time be taken in reviewing cases so as to
avoid mistakes.

Recently, large numbers of cases have passed
through the Special Board of the People's
Commissar of Internal Affairs of the USSR, and at
each session of the Special Commission [*osoboe
soveshchanie*], from 200 to 300 cases are reviewed.

In such a situation, the possibility of making
erroneous decisions cannot be excluded.

I presented my thoughts about this to c. Beria, along
with a suggestion to establish an operating
procedure of work of the Special Board in which its

meetings are scheduled more often, and with fewer
numbers of cases to be reviewed at each session.

I would consider it expedient if the Commissariat of
Internal Affairs received special instructions from
the TsK VKP(b) and the SNK USSR about this
matter.

A. Vyshinskii (Lubianka 1939-1946 94-95 No. 50)

As late as October 28, 1939, a group of prosecutors (*prokurory*)
wrote to Andrei Zhdanov to ask him to intercede with the Central
Committee about the slowness of the NKVD to review cases of persons innocently imprisoned. They complained that the new Chief
Prosecutor of the USSR, Mikhail Ivanovich Pankrat'ev, was weak
and deferred too much to Commissar of the NKVD Beria, who was
also a Politburo member.

The party's Central Committee decision of
November 17, 1938, identified the grossest
distortions of Soviet laws by NKVD organs and
obligated those organs and the Procuracy **not only
to stop these crimes but also to correct the gross
violations of law that have resulted in mass
sentencing of totally innocent, honest Soviet
persons to various sorts of punishment, often
even execution. These persons — not a few, but
tens and hundreds of thousands — sit in camps
and jails and wait for a just decision**; they are
perplexed about why and for what they were
arrested and **by what right the bastards from
Ezhov's band persecuted them, using medieval
torture.**

It would seem that the party's Central Committee
decision of November 17, 1938, should have
mobilized all attention on **immediately rectifying
the criminal policy of the bastard Ezhov and his
criminal clique, which has literally terrorized
Soviet persons, upright, dedicated citizens, old
party members, and entire party organizations.**

In reality, something else is happening.

> Comrade Pankrat'ev, who has replaced Comrade
> Vyshinskii, cannot guarantee implementation of
> this critical decision of the party Central Committee
> because of his lack of authority in the Procuracy
> and particularly in the eyes of NKVD personnel.
> (Koenker & Bachman 26-27)[5]

The prosecutors end by asking for Pankrat'ev's recall since he did not have enough authority, and – for a raise in pay for themselves, the prosecutors. This last request imparts a somewhat subjective tone to their letter.

But there is no doubt that the review of cases was slow. Beria, after all, could not fire all the NKVD men who had worked under Ezhov and, before him, under Iagoda. And in every locality, the NKVD men must have been cautious about reversing verdicts based on investigations that their predecessors, colleagues, or even themselves, had performed.

The strongly anticommunist scholar Valerii Vasiliev admits that Beria's exonerations also took place in the Ukrainian SSR:

> The absurd nature of the case [an alleged rebel
> group in Poltava oblast'] was so evident that in
> 1939 the majority of those arrested were released
> and completely rehabilitated. (Vasiliev, Terror 157)

Vasiliev is in error in assuming that clearly "absurd" charges would prevent unjust convictions. Of course this is not true. Ezhov and his men repressed and executed a great many people without any evidence at all!

Beria, and Stalin and the Politburo, really were trying to undo those of Ezhov's injustices they could. Vasiliev simply does not wish to admit this. Meanwhile, on the same page Vasiliev concedes

---

[5] Online at
https://msuweb.montclair.edu/~furrg/research/prosecutors_zhdanov_102839.pdf

that A. Volkov, one of the authors of mass repressions in the Ukrainian SSR, had been arrested March 9, 1939, and was executed October 16, 1941 – that is, under Beria.

Ezhov's Confessions

All ideologically anticommunist accounts suppress the evidence of Ezhov's conspiracy against the Soviet government. None of them refers to the confessions of Ezhov and his men, though these confessions have long been available to them.

The apparent reason for the failure to discuss Ezhov's conspiracy is the desire on the part of anticommunist researchers to falsely accuse Stalin of having ordered all the huge number of executions carried out by Ezhov. But Ezhov explicitly states many times that his repressions and executions were carried out in pursuit of his own private conspiratorial goals and that he had deceived the Soviet government.

Thus Ezhov's own confessions are evidence that Stalin and the central Soviet leadership were not responsible for his massive executions. There is no evidence that these confessions represent anything but what Ezhov chose to say – no evidence of torture, threats, or fabrication.

In his confession of August 4, 1939 Ezhov specifically states that he deceived the Soviet government about the extent and nature of espionage: "[W]e were deceiving the government in the most blatant manner." Ezhov's confessions that he deceived the government for his conspiratorial purposes are not contradicted by any other evidence.

The only conclusion supported by the evidence contradicts the "anti-Stalin" ideological aims of these anticommunist researchers. But it is important – in fact, indispensable -- to them that Stalin and the Soviet leadership be "guilty" of "mass murders." It is vital to them that Ezhov be nothing but "Stalin's loyal executioner." It is essential that Stalin be a "dictator" who could control everything with a word. So they omit evidence, such as Ezhov's confessions, that tends to disprove this preconceived, and erroneous, notion.

To concede that Ezhov was not acting under Stalin's orders or ful-
filling Stalin's wishes, but just the opposite, would mean conceding
that Ezhov was *not* "Stalin's loyal executioner," "Stalin's nursling
(*pitomets*)." It would dismantle the "anti-Stalin paradigm" of Soviet
history. Acceptance of this paradigm is a requirement in mainstream Soviet history, and the evidence be damned!

Jansen and Petrov quote from an interrogation of Uspenskii, one of
Ezhov's NKVD accomplices:

> In Kiev, the group carried out large-scale arrests,
> with Ezhov, never sober, approving without looking
> into the matter. Uspenskii was astonished and
> alarmed by his drunken table talk. **During the trip,**
> **Ezhov drank uninterruptedly, boasting to**
> **Uspenskii that he had the Politburo "in his**
> **hands" and could do literally anything, arrest**
> **anyone, including Politburo members**. (Case of
> Uspenskii) (Jansen & Petrov, 133)

Some pages later they outline Ezhov's plan for a *putsch*, a violent
seizure of power planned for November 7, 1938.

> He [Ezhov] testified himself that after arrests began
> within the NKVD he, together with Frinovskii,
> Dagin, and Evdokimov, made **plans to commit a**
> **"putsch" on 7 November**, the October Revolution
> anniversary, during the demonstration in Red
> Square. The plan was to cause a commotion and
> then in the panic and confusion to "drop bombs and
> kill someone of the government members." (Jansen
> & Petrov, 155)

They continue with yet more evidence of Ezhov's plot to kill Stalin:

> Evdokimov gave similar evidence. According to
> him, in September he discussed the threatening
> situation after Beria's appointment with Ezhov,
> Frinovskii, and Bel'skii. **Allegedly, they agreed to**
> **prepare an attempt on Stalin and Molotov.**
> **Ezhov was also said to have had plans to murder**
> **Beria**.... According to Iu. K. Ivanov, an NKVD

> executive from Evdokimov's circle, as early as late July, after a visit to Ezhov, **Evdokimov had alluded to terrorism against the Party leadership**. (Jansen & Petrov, 156)

> According to Konstantinov, sometime in mid-November Ezhov told him that his song was ended, thanks to Stalin and loyal Stalinists like his deputy Beria: "If they could be removed, all would be different." **He suggested that Konstantinov should kill Stalin**, but without giving any concrete form to his plans. (Jansen & Petrov, 156)

Yet Jansen and Petrov insist that Ezhov was "loyal" to Stalin. They insist on asserting the anti-Stalin paradigm, in defiance of the evidence they themselves provide.

The editors of one of the important document collections write the following:

> I.Ia. Dagin was arrested on November 5 1938, before Ezhov's removal from the position of Commissar of Internal Affairs. Dagin was one of the workers in the central apparatus of the NKVD who was closest to Ezhov. In the confessions of all of the arrested leading workers in the NKVD he figures as one of the main participants in **the so-called conspiracy in the NKVD. At the beginning of 1939 Stalin regularly read the transcripts of the interrogations of the leadership of the NKVD and it is possible that he really believed that there was a conspiracy in the organs of state security**. ...Dagin's position as chief of the security section was considered one of the most important of those in the operative sections of the GUGB and Stalin read his confessions concerning the conspiracy. (Lubianka 1939-1946, 564)

Obviously Stalin did *not* think that Ezhov was his "loyal executioner." Yet the editors, writing 65 years later and with much less evidence than Stalin had, call this "the so-called conspiracy."

In the following chapters we will examine Ezhov's and Frinovskii's confessions at some length. We will also outline the method that should be used for evaluating these confessions.

Chapter 11. Frinovskii's Statement to Beria April 11, 1939

In this chapter we examine the confession statement by Ezhov's deputy, Mikhail Frinovskii. This statement and the confessions and interrogations we will analyze in the following chapters are essential evidence for an accurate understanding of Soviet high politics of the 1930s. They are ignored by almost all professional students of Soviet history on ideological grounds alone.[1]

According to the "official version" of Soviet history of the Stalin period – what we call the "anti-Stalin paradigm":

* Stalin was a "dictator."

* The opposition conspiracies revealed in the Moscow Trials and Tukhachevskii Affair were frame-ups of innocent people. The bloc of oppositionists disclosed in all these trials never existed. And all such revelations and confessions were the result of torture and/or threats.

Once these positions are accepted *a priori* it follows that the mass repression of 1937-1938 must have been Stalin's plan. It would also follow – again, from this wrong *a priori* assumption – that Stalin could have stopped the mass repressions whenever he chose to do so. He could have done so earlier, or he could have chosen not to have mass repressions at all. It also follows that Stalin must have shifted the blame to Ezhov and his men, making them his scapegoats when all they had been doing was carrying out his orders as they understood them.

But all this is nonsense. It directly contradicts *all* the evidence we now have — and we have a great deal of it. But this preconceived

---

[1] Ideology is not a category opposed to evidence. Rather, ideology shapes how evidence is interpreted. Ideology bereft of evidence is prejudice, not an attempt to discover the truth.

conclusion is demanded by the prevailing model of Soviet history, the "anti-Stalin paradigm."

In this chapter we will examine Frinovskii's confession statement addressed to Lavrentii P. Beria. As of this writing (June 2016) this is the only document from Frinovskii's investigation file that has been made public. We will cite quotations from this document. The full texts in both Russian and English are online for those who wish to study them more closely. (Frinovskii) Throughout this chapter quotations are from Frinovskii's statement unless otherwise noted.

Frinovskii's Statement of April 11, 1939

Mikhail Petrovich Frinovskii had been replaced as Ezhov's deputy by Beria on April 22, 1938. He was arrested on April 6, 1938 and made a comprehensive statement five days later. Frinovskii's most significant revelations in it concern the different conspiracies against the Soviet government and the Stalin leadership and his own and Ezhov's involvement in them.

> At that same time, 1934, I had several meetings with [Efim Georgievich] Evdokimov[2] when he came to Moscow. At these meetings he gradually disclosed to me his practical work and spoke about the work of the center of the Rights and around the USSR. In particular he told me that he had a number of people inside the apparatus of the GPU, and named Rud', Dagin, Raev, Kurskii, Dement'ev, Gorbach, and others. He said that he was beginning to have contacts in the national oblasts: in Dagestan, though Mamedbekov, in Chechnya – Gorsheev or Gorshenin, and then said that the only person he had trouble with was Kalmykov, who had his own line of work, and Evdokimov couldn't cut

---

[2] Wheatcroft's 2007 article gives biographical information about Evdokimov. He was active in the Cheka and GPU until 1934 when he went into Party work, serving as First Secretary of several different areas. Frinovskii notes that Evdokimov was close to Ezhov and to himself. Evdokimov was ultimately tried and executed at the same time as many other Ezhov men in the NKVD and Ezhov himself, in late January to early February 1940.

him off in any way, but he characterized Kalmykov as a man wholly "ours," a Rightist, but evidently one who had his own line of work.

I asked him what was being done generally in the USSR? Evdokimov said that large-scale work was going on, a whole number of people who had important positions in a number of other oblasts of the USSR, had crossed over to the Rights. And here he stated: "You see how we must now conduct the struggle with the Central Committee: at one time we fought against the movement of uprisings, and now we ourselves must seek out the threads, ties to this movement and, in order to organize it, we must go down to its base. This is very complicated and dangerous work but without the base – the secretaries of the regional committees, the chairmen of the regional executive committees (RIKs) or men who have contacts with the countryside – we will not be able to lead the movement of uprisings, and that is one of the fundamental tasks that presents itself to us." (38)

The above passage makes it clear that by 1934 the Rights had recruited many local Party leaders and were planning to recruit more of them. This constitutes important evidence that many Party leaders were in fact involved in the far-flung "bloc" of Rights, Trotskyists, and other oppositionists.

In his "Secret Speech" to the XX Party Congress in 1956 Nikita Khrushchev revealed that a great many delegates to the XVII Party Congress in January 1934 were executed within the next several years. Khrushchev falsely implied that they were all innocent victims of frame-ups. He arranged for many of them to be "rehabilitated" and others were later rehabilitated under Gorbachev.

Extracts from Evdokimov's case are given in a report dated February 9, 1956 in the document collection *Reabilitatsiia. Kak Eto Bylo. Mart 1953 – Fevral' 1956*. (RKEB 1) The section of this report titled "On the 'conspiracies' in the Organs of the NKVD" (RKEB

1,339 ff.) notes that "Beria arrested [many NKVD men] and stated that he was liquidating a conspiracy headed by Ezhov, Frinovskii, and Evdokimov." (340)

In *Khrushchev Lied* we analyzed a number of Khrushchev-era "re-habilitation" reports and showed that they are dishonest "white-washes" that, moreover, do not in fact demonstrate the innocence of those "rehabilitated." Others like Matthew Lenoe have shown that Khrushchev and his men lied about the events of the 1930s.

Frinovskii continues:

> At one of these meetings during horseback riding Lifshits said to me: "I heard about you from Evdokimov. Frankly, I did not suspect that you were also with us. Good for you!" I began to speak with Lifshits – and how about you? He answered: **"Evdokimov has already told you that I am doing work."** I asked him again – are you doing important work? He said that he was doing important work, **he had contact with the conspiratorial center through Piatakov**, had a large number of people and was not breaking his contacts with the Ukrainians. (39)

Iakov Abramovich Lifshits, along with Iurii Piatakov, was to be a defendant in the January 1937 Moscow Trial of the "Anti-Soviet Trotskyite Center." Lifshits confessed his guilt, was convicted, and executed on February 1, 1937.

Deribas

Frinovskii:

> I had that conversation with **Deribas**, and Deribas was interested, in the main, in the names of the people who had already been repressed and the people who were mentioned in the [investigative] materials. **I told him about Lifshits and Piatakov who were on the point of being exposed.** (41)

Terentii Dmitrievich Deribas was head of the NKVD in the Far Eastern region. He was arrested by Genrikh S. Liushkov on Ezhov's orders, tried, convicted, and shot "for espionage, Trotskyism, and organizing a series of conspiracies in the NKVD and the Red Army."[3] Deribas was rehabilitated under Khrushchev in 1957.

But Liushkov told his Japanese handlers that Deribas was in fact guilty.

> According to Lyushkov, the interrogations of **Deribas**, Zapadni, and Barminski established that in the NKVD and the border guard forces, a plot centering on Gamarnik had been fomented. **For a long time Deribas had been in contact with Rykov and was the latter's 'hidden conspirator'.** In concert with Lavrenty Lavrentiev (former First Secretary of the Regional Committee of the Party until January 1937), with Grigory Krutov (shot in April 1938), and with the army plotters Sangurski, Aronshtam, and others, **Deribas supposedly intended to conduct a putsch in the Far East and to reach agreement with the Japanese for help and for combined operations against the Soviet Union.** (Coox, Lesser 1, 156)

Liushkov was in Japan. So we have good evidence from a source outside the Soviet Union that Deribas was in fact guilty! This is not only further evidence that Khrushchev's rehabilitations are dishonest – we know that already from many sources. More important for us here, it is evidence that confirms and is consistent with Frinovskii's statement.

Eikhe

> At one of my meetings in 1935 Evdokimov at his apartment told me about a number of men whom he had drawn into the work in Pyatigorsk. He

---

[3] Russian Wikipedia page on Deribas at https://ru.wikipedia.org/wiki/
Дерибас,_Терентий_Дмитриевич

named Pivovarov and a large group of Chekists:
Boiar, Diatkin, and Shatskii. Here too he told me
about his contacts with Khataevich, and also
praised him in every way as a man who knew the
countryside; **with Eikhe**, about part of the
Leningrad group... (40)

Robert Indrikovich Eikhe was First Secretary of the Western Siberia region. As we have seen in an earlier chapter, it was Eikhe
who first requested the extraordinary powers that, when given to
other First Secretaries, became the "kulak operation" and then the
Ezhovshchina.[4]

According to documents available to Jansen and Petrov, many of
which have since been reclassified by the Russian government and
are no longer available to researchers, Eikhe interfered in NKVD
matters, insisting on the arrest of persons against whom there was
no evidence. Ezhov told his subordinates not to oppose Eikhe but
to cooperate with him.

Consider the objections raised at the time of the
July 1937 Moscow conference by the Western
Siberian NKVD chief, Mironov, to Ezhov against the
First Party secretary, Robert Eikhe. Mironov
reported to Ezhov—according to his testimony
after arrest— that Eikhe "interfered in NKVD
affairs." **He had ordered the chiefs of the Kuzbass
NKVD town branches to arrest Party members,
although in most cases evidence was missing.**
Mironov thought his position difficult: either he had
to liberate part of the prisoners and clash with
Eikhe, or the NKVD organs were forced to "create
fictitious cases." When Mironov suggested to orally
instruct the NKVD organs concerned only to carry
out orders approved by him, **Ezhov answered:**

---

[4] Khrushchev famously quoted from a letter by Eikhe to Beria in 1939 in which Eikhe re-
peatedly declares his innocence and protests that he has been badly beaten by Ezhov's men.
I have studied this letter and reprinted the whole text, including the parts omitted by
Khrushchev, in Furr, Khrushchev.

> **"Eikhe knows what he is doing.** He is responsible
> for the Party organization; it is useless to fight with
> him. You better report to me the moot points
> arising, and I will settle them. . . . **Comply with
> Eikhe's instructions,** and don't strain your
> relations with him." (Jansen & Petrov, 91)

This is consistent with Frinovskii's statement about the way
Ezhov, and he himself, operated – beating and framing innocent
persons in order to appear to be fighting a conspiracy while hiding
their own conspiracy. Frinovskii's statement, together with the
documents quoted by Jansen and Petrov, are strong evidence that
Eikhe was indeed involved in a Rightist conspiracy.

The Conspiracy of the Rights

> Before the arrest of Bukharin and Rykov Ezhov,
> speaking with me openly, started to talk about the
> plans for Chekist work in connection with the
> current situation and **the imminent arrests of
> Bukharin and Rykov. Ezhov said that this would
> be a great loss to the Rights,** after that regardless
> of our own wishes, upon the instructions of the
> Central Committee large-scale measures might be
> taken against the cadres of the Right, and that in
> connection with this **his and my main task must
> be to direct the investigation in such a way so
> that, as much as possible, to preserve the
> Rightist cadre.**

> ... In carrying out this suggestion of Ezhov's **we
> chose a firm course in preserving Yagoda's
> cadres in leading posts in the NKVD.** It is
> essential to mention that we only managed to do
> this with difficulty, since **in various local organs
> [of the NKVD] there were materials on the
> majority of these people about their
> participation in the conspiracy and in anti-
> Soviet work generally.** (42)

Here Frinovskii makes it clear that the Moscow Trials were not fabrications but genuine. He mentions Piatakov's guilt, and that of Zinoviev and Kamenev.

> Evdokimov swore, spit, and said: "Can't you get me into the NKVD, I'll be able to help more than the rest." **Ezhov said**: "It would be good, but the Central Committee will scarcely agree to transfer you to the NKVD. I think that the situation is not altogether hopeless, but you need to have a talk with Dagin, you have influence on him, it's necessary for him to develop the work in the operations department, and **we need to be prepared to carry out terrorist acts.**" (43)

Ezhov's discussing the need for "terror" – meaning assassination – is consistent with Ezhov's own confessions that he attempted to assassinate Stalin and other Politburo members, in part at the urging of the Germans.

> ... here Evdokimov and Ezhov together talked about the possible limiting of the operations but, as this was considered impossible, **they agreed to deflect the blow from their own cadre and to try to direct to against honest cadres who were devoted to the Central Committee.** That was Ezhov's instruction. (44)

This is consistent with Ezhov's later confessions that an important part of his conspiracy was to kill a great many people loyal to the Soviet leadership, and many more who were simply innocent, in order to weaken the Soviet state and sow discontent with it among the population. The hope was that this would facilitate uprisings against the Soviet government in the event of a German or Japanese invasion, thus helping Ezhov and his accomplices to seize power.

> In the autumn of 1935 at Lifshits' dacha a meeting between Evdokimov, myself, Dagin, and Lifshits took place, at which Evdokimov in an extremely irritated condition began to say that he did not have

> confidence at all in the success of the terrorist acts
> that were under preparation by Trotskyites and
> Rights against Stalin. Evdokimov then directly
> stated that a terrorist act against Stalin could only
> be realistically carried out by the forces of the
> security department of the NKVD. (44)

We have independent evidence of Trotsky's and Sedov's dedication to "terror" (assassination), and also that of the Rights. (Furr, Amalgams) Frinovskii's statement confirms that evidence. It also makes sense. Unlike the political activists and Party malcontents in the bloc of oppositionists, NKVD forces were trained in the use of violence.

Other Important Aspects of Frinovskii's Statement

The following section of this chapter concerns the falsification of cases against innocent persons for the purposes of massive repression.

The Falsification of Cases

Frinovskii's discussion of massive falsification of cases against innocent persons, including the fabrication of false case files and the torture of prisoners, deserves quoting at length.

> The investigative apparatus in all departments of
> the NKVD was divided into "investigator-
> bonebreakers," "bonebreakers," and "ordinary"
> investigators.
>
> What did these groups represent and who were
> they?
>
> **"Investigator-bonebreakers" were chosen
> basically from among the conspirators or
> persons who were compromised. They had
> unsupervised recourse to beating arrested
> persons and in a very short time obtained
> "confessions" and knew how to write up
> transcripts in a grammatical and elegant
> fashion.**

In this category belong: Nikolayev, Agas, Ushakov, Listengurt, Evgen'ev, Zhupakhin, Minaev, Davydov, Al'tman, Geiman, Litvin, Leplevskii, Karelin, Kerzon, Iamnitskii, and others.

Since the quantity of those under arrest who confessed due to such methods grew daily and there was a great need for investigators who knew how to compose interrogations, the so-called "investigator-bonebreakers" began, each on his own, to create groups of simple "bonebreakers."

The group of "bonebreakers" consisted of technical workers. These men did not know the evidence concerning the suspect, but were sent to the Lefortovo [prison in Moscow], summoned the accused, and set to beating him. The beatings continued up to the moment that the accused agreed to give a confession.

The remaining group of investigators took care of interrogations of those accused of less serious crimes and were left to themselves, without leadership from anyone.

The further process of investigation was as follows: the investigator conducted the interrogation and instead of a transcript put together notes. After several such interrogations a draft transcript was put together by the investigator. The draft went for "correction" to the chief of the appropriate department, and from him, still unsigned, for "review" to former People's Commissar Ezhov and in rare cases to myself. Ezhov looked through the transcript, made changes and additions. **In most cases those under arrest did not agree with the editing of the transcript and stated that they had not said that during the investigation and refused to sign it.**

Then the investigators would remind the arrested party about the "bonebreakers," and the person under investigation would sign the transcript. Ezhov produced the "correction" and "editing" of transcripts, in most cases, never having seen with his own eyes the person under arrest and if he did see him, then only during a momentary inspection of the cells or investigative rooms.

With such methods the investigations supplied the names.

In my opinion I would speak the truth if I declared, in general, that very often the confessions were given by the investigators, and not by those under investigation.

Did the leadership of the People's Commissariat, that is I and Ezhov, know about this? We knew.

How did we react? Honestly speaking – not at all, and Ezhov even encouraged it. No one bothered to find out to which of the accused physical pressure was applied. And since the majority of the persons who were employing these methods were themselves enemies of the people and conspirators, then clearly false accusations took place, **we took false accusations and arrested and shot innocent people who had been slandered by enemies of the people from among those under arrest and by enemies of the people among the investigators. Real investigation was wiped out**. (45-46)

Since the end of the Soviet Union a large body of evidence has been published that alleges the torture of innocent persons to force them to confess. Here Frinovskii verifies that this practice was a policy of the Ezhov-led NKVD. It cannot be impugned because the fabrication of false cases against and torture of innocent persons is confirmed by so much independent evidence.

Frinovskii's testimony also confirms Ezhov's confessions, which we will examine in subsequent chapters. It is also strong evidence that Ezhov's NKVD acted not under Stalin's orders but against them.

Frinovskii Confirms the Guilt of Bukharin and Defendants at the Third Moscow Trial

Frinovskii explicitly states that the Third Moscow Trial was **not** fabricated, that the defendants were **not** forced to confess to crimes they did not commit. This is very significant. In the following passage Frinovskii states that Ezhov did not force Bukharin and others to falsely confess. Instead he asked them not to name him as one of the Rightist conspirators – and Bukharin and the others did not.

> The preparation of the trial of Rykov, Bukharin, Krestinskii, Yagoda and others
>
> An active participant in investigations generally, **Ezhov kept himself aloof from the preparation of this trial. Before the trial the face-to-face confrontations of the suspects, interrogations, and refining, in which Ezhov did not participate.** He spoke for a long time with Yagoda, and that talk concerned, in the main, of assuring Yagoda that he would not be shot.
>
> Ezhov had conversations several times with Bukharin and Rykov and also in order to calm them assured them that under no circumstances would they be shot.
>
> Ezhov had one conversation with Bulanov, and began this conversation in the presence of the investigator and myself, and finished the conversation one on one, having asked us to leave.

At that moment Bulanov had begun talking about the poisoning of Ezhov. What the conversation was about Ezhov did not say. When he asked us to enter again he said: "Behave yourself well at the trial – I will ask that you not be shot." After the trial Ezhov always expressed regret about Bulanov. At the time of the executions Ezhov suggested shooting Bulanov first and he himself did not enter the building where the shootings took place.

Here Ezhov unquestionably was ruled by the necessity of covering up his own ties with the arrested leaders of the Right who were going into the public trial. (47-48)

We have a great deal of other evidence that Bukharin was guilty. This evidence also serves as confirmation of the genuine nature of Frinovskii's statement.

Chapter 12. Ezhov's Interrogation of April 26, 1939

Ezhov was arrested on April 10, 1939. As in the case of Frinovskii we do not have his entire file with every interrogation and statement. We have excerpts from two earlier interrogations which we will touch upon briefly in a future chapter. The text of this specific interrogation appears to be complete. Like Frinovskii's, it is published in a semi-official collection of declassified documents from Soviet archives.

The central focus of this interrogation is Ezhov's collaboration with the German military in a conspiracy to overthrow the Stalin leadership.

> Question: At the last interrogation you confessed that over the period of ten years you carried out espionage work for Poland. However, you hid a number of your espionage contacts. The investigation demands from you truthful and exhaustive confessions on this question.
>
> Answer: I must admit that, **although I gave truthful confessions about my espionage work for Poland, I really did hide from the investigation my espionage ties with the Germans.**
>
> Question: With what aims did you try to lead the investigation away from your espionage ties with the Germans.
>
> Answer: I did not want to confess to the investigation about my direct espionage ties with the Germans, all the more since my collaboration with German intelligence is not limited only to espionage work assigned by German intelligence, **I**

organized an anti-Soviet conspiracy and was preparing a coup d'état by means of terrorist acts against the leaders of the party and government. (Ezhov 04.26.1939, 52-53)

Ezhov explains how he was blackmailed by German intelligence, a claim that the interrogator finds difficult to believe.

Question: **The conditions of your recruitment by German intelligence that you have related do not inspire belief.**

It is incomprehensible and strange that you should have agreed to be recruited when all you had to fear was publicity in the foreign press about your intimate relationship with some woman.

Speak plainly: how did German intelligence get its claws into you?

This statement by the interrogator is good internal evidence that Ezhov's confession was not "scripted" in any way by the NKVD but represents what Ezhov himself wished to say. We should recall that Iakov Iakovlev stated that the Germans also used blackmail against him.

Answer: At that time I had only just been promoted to important political work. Publicity about this incident would have discredited me in the USSR and possibly led to the exposure of my personal depravity. Besides that, before this, as the investigation is aware, I had already been tied with Polish intelligence, so there was nothing for me to lose. (54)

Austrian Doctor Carl von Noorden's clinic in Vienna was indeed visited by many high-ranking Bolsheviks. Ezhov names some of these patients of von Noorden's:

Answer: At the beginning of 1936 upon the recommendation of the medical directorate of the Kremlin Noorden was invited to Moscow for

consultation with a number of high-ranking
workers. He stayed in the USSR for 10 – 15 days.

**Of the large number of persons whom Noorden
consulted I specifically remember Gamarnik,
Iakir, Chubar', Petrovsky, Kosior, Veinberg, and
Metallikov.** (57)

Gavriil Veinberg was a Soviet Trade Union official. Mikhail Metallikov, a surgeon, was himself the director of Kremlin medical facili-
ties. With the exception of Veinberg, all those named by Ezhov
here were eventually arrested, tried, and executed for participation in anti-Soviet conspiracy.[1]

Ezhov testifies in detail about his contacts with General Kurt von
Hammerstein-Equord. Hammerstein was a partisan of an alliance
with Russia but not with the Stalin leadership. At least two of his
children were secret members of the German Communist Party.
He was on friendly terms with the Soviet Generals who had visited
Germany during the Soviet-German collaboration under the Treaty
of Rapallo.

> On the fifth or sixth day of my stay in Merano
> Kandelaki informed me that **the prominent
> German general Hammerstein had arrived** at
> our sanatorium in the company of the Polish
> minister of trade whose name I cannot now recall.
> (58)

Ezhov describes the different pro-German groups of high-ranking
Red Army commanders that were conspiring against the Stalin
leadership but were unable to unite.

> At the beginning of our talk **Hammerstein
> declared: "We are very grateful for all the
> services you have rendered us."** He declared that

---

[1] There is an article on von Noorden's Bolshevik patients in the Russian business newspaper
Kommersant at http://www.kommersant.ru/doc/761081 It does not mention the blackmail
and recruitment of von Noorden's patients by German intelligence. Von Noorden's life and
career are summarized on a German Wikipedia page at
https://de.wikipedia.org/wiki/Carl_von_Noorden_(Mediziner)

he was satisfied with the information that the Germans had received from me. But, declared Hammerstein, it was all trivial stuff! **The position in the USSR that you occupy is such that we cannot be satisfied with the information that you are giving us. Before you stand other assignments of a political order."**

Question: What kind of "political" assignments?

Answer: Hammerstein, knowing that I had already been elected secretary of the Central Committee of the ACP(b), declared: **"You have the possibility not just to inform us but also to influence the policy of Soviet power."**

Further **Hammerstein made known to me the very serious, in his words, relations that the Germans had in the circles of the high command of the Red Army, and informed me of the existence in the Soviet Union of several military-conspiratorial groups.**

Hammerstein told me that a number of high-ranking military workers were dissatisfied with the situation in the USSR and had set as their goal to change the internal and international policies of the Soviet Union. (59)

Hammerstein answered: "We have relations with different circles among your military. Their goal is the same but, evidently, their points of view are different, and they cannot reach any agreement amongst themselves even though we have categorically demanded it."

Question: What assignments did Hammerstein give you?

Answer: **Hammerstein proposed that I contact these military circles, and with Egorov first of all.** He declared that he knew Egorov very well as one of the most important and influential figures among **that part of the military conspirators who understood that without the German army, without a solid agreement with Germany it would not be possible to change the political order in the USSR in the desired direction.**

The view that any conspiracy had to have a prior agreement with Germany was also set forth by Trotsky to Radek and Piatakov. It made a lot of sense. The overthrow of the Stalin leadership or assassination of Stalin would certainly create profound disorder and disunity in the country. Some agreement with the most aggressive imperialist countries would be needed so they would recognize the new regime rather than invade and permanently occupy large parts of the USSR.

Hammerstein proposed to me that **through Egorov I should be current with all the conspiratorial matters and influence the conspiratorial groups that existed in the Red Army in the direction of bringing them close to Germany** while at the same time taking every step towards their "unification." "Your position as secretary of the CC ACP(b) will help you in this," declared Hammerstein. (59)

Question: Did your further meetings with Hammerstein take place?

Answer: Yes, I had three more meetings with Hammerstein. At the second meeting **Hammerstein expressed interest in the details related to the murder of S.M. Kirov, and about how serious the influence of Trotskyites, Zinovievites and Rights in the ACP(b) was.**

I gave him exhaustive information, and specifically noted the fact that there was at that time a sense of despair among Chekists and that Iagoda's position in connection with Kirov's murder had been shaken. Then Hammerstein said: **"It would be very good if you managed to occupy Iagoda's post."** (59-60)

According to Ezhov's account, it seems as though Hammerstein was already considering what a useful role the NKVD could play in undermining the Soviet leadership if it were under the command of a German agent like Ezhov.

Ezhov then outlined the various conspiratorial groupings among the leading Soviet military commanders.

Answer: In the conversation with Hammerstein **it was agreed that I would maintain communications with him through Egorov and Kandelaki,** during the latter's trips to Moscow.

On a non-workday he [Egorov] came to my dacha and the first conversation took place in which **Egorov told me that he already knew about my meeting with Hammerstein, with whom he himself had long had ties.** ... Egorov further gave me the names of the participants of the conspiratorial group that he led: Budennyi, Dybenko, Shaposhnikov, Kashirin, Fed'ko, the commander of the Transbaikal military district, and a number of other important commanders whose names I will remember and give in a supplement.

Further Egorov said that **in the RKKA there exist two more groups competing with each other: the Trotskyist group of Gamarnik, Iakir and Uborevich, and the officer-Bonapartist group of Tukhachevsky.** (61)

In his letter to Marshal Voroshilov after the Tukhachevskii trial and executions Marshal Semion Budennyi also noted that a distinction between the pro-Trotsky commanders and Tukhachevskii's group was expressed during the Tukhachevskii trial of June 11, 1937. This confirms the genuine nature of Ezhov's confession here.

Understandably, the Germans were unhappy with the divisions among the different groups of military conspirators. They demanded unity – in vain, as it turned out.

> Then [German military attaché to the Soviet Union General Ernst] **Köstring** informed me that **my appointment as People's Commissar of Internal Affairs opened up the perspective "of uniting all those dissatisfied with the existing political leadership and that, at the head of this movement**, I would be able to create a considerable force."

> Köstring said: "We military men think like this: for us the decisive factor is military strength. Therefore **the first task which, as it seems to us, presents itself is to unite the military forces in the interests of the common task.** We must strengthen in every way our influence in the Red Army, **so as to direct the Russian army at the decisive moment in a manner corresponding to the interests of Germany."**

How Ezhov's Mass Repression Originated

According to Ezhov the idea of an NKVD conspiracy was first suggested to him by German military attaché General Ernst Köstring.

> Köstring touched on the NKVD. He said: "In the general plan of the tasks we face, the People's Commissar for Internal Affairs must play a determining role. Therefore **for the success of the coup d'état and our seizure of power you must create in the NKVD a broad organization of those who agree with you,** and it must be **united with the military men."** Köstring declared that these organizations, in the army and in the NKVD,

must be prepared in such a way as **to guarantee united actions at the outbreak of war towards the goal of seizing power.** (62)

After the Tukhachevsky Affair trial and executions, Egorov and the Germans reconsidered this original plan, which was oriented towards action upon an invasion of the USSR by Germany and/or allies. With the top figures in the military conspiracy now removed, the Germans suggested a *coup d'état* instead of the initial plan of coordinating Red Army actions with an invading German army.

> Question: How did your espionage work proceed further?
>
> Answer: In the summer of 1937, after the trial of Tukhachevsky, Egorov in the name of German intelligence set before me the question of **the necessity to build all the espionage work in the army and the NKVD in such a way as to organize, under certain conditions, the seizure of power without waiting for a war,** as we had agreed according to the preliminary plan.
>
> Egorov said that **the Germans explained this alteration by the fear lest the destruction which had begun of the anti-Soviet formations in the army** reach us, i.e. me and Egorov.
>
> According to Egorov the Germans proposed that we communicate to them our concrete ideas about this question as soon as possible.
>
> We discussed this new situation with Egorov and arrived at the conclusion that **the Party and the popular masses were behind the leadership of the ACP(b) and that the soil for this coup d'état had not been prepared.** Therefore we decided that **it was necessary to get rid of Stalin or Molotov** under the flag of some other kind of anti-Soviet organization in order to create the

conditions for my further advancement towards political power. After that, **once I occupied a more leading position**, the possibility would be created for **further, more decisive, changes in the politics of the Party and the Soviet Union that corresponded to the interests of Germany.**

I asked Egorov to transmit to the Germans through Köstring our ideas and to request the opinion of governmental circles in Germany about this question.

Question: What answer did you receive?

Answer: Soon after that, according to the words of Köstring, Egorov informed me that **the government circles of Germany agreed with our proposal.**

According to Ezhov, it was at this time that his plan of an NKVD conspiracy was born.

Question: What measures did you undertake to realize your traitorous designs?

Answer: **I decided to organize a conspiracy within the NKVD and to attract to it people through whom I could carry out terrorist acts against the leaders of the Party and government.** (64)

The NKVD conspiracy was to include terrorist acts against the Stalin leadership.

Ezhov goes on to name those in the NKVD, plus Evdokimov (not an NKVD man), who were already in his conspiratorial group, including a group of NKVD men who had been in Iagoda's conspiracy. In later confessions Ezhov goes into detail about how the mass repressions were planned and executed. We will discuss them in future chapters.

The final section of this confession details the plot to assassinate Stalin. Marshal Egorov was arrested on March 27, 1938. In one of the document collections which we have cited previously, we have a Politburo decision of January 25, 1938 detailing suspicious actions by Egorov. Marshal Budennyi had evidently testified that Egorov had tried to recruit him into an anti-party military conspiracy of his own. A number of persons already under arrest had testified that Egorov knew about the Tukhachevskii conspiracy but had failed to denounce it to the Soviet leadership. (Lubianka 1937-1938 No. 281)

A decree of the Central Committee Plenum dated February 28 – March 2, 1938 reported that Egorov had had a face-to-face confrontation with four of his accusers and concluded that "com[rade]. Egorov has turned out to be politically more tarnished than one could have thought before the face-to-face confrontation." At this point Egorov was only removed as a candidate member of the Central Committee. (Lubianka 1937-1938 No. 297).

In a list dated July 26, 1938, of 139 persons for whom the NKVD recommended execution if convicted at trial, Egorov's was the only name crossed out entirely. (Lubianka 1937-1938 No. 331). Egorov was not tried and executed until February 22, 1939, long after Beria had taken charge of the NKVD from Ezhov and embarked on the task of reviewing the cases of tens of thousands of persons condemned under Ezhov.

Egorov's arrest caused a change in Ezhov's plans.

> I informed Köstring about further arrests among military workers and declared to him that I did not have the power to prevent these arrests, and in particular **I reported about the arrest of Egorov, which had the possibility of causing the ruin of the whole conspiracy.**
>
> Köstring was extremely upset by all these events. He sharply put to me the question that **either we immediately take some kind of measures to seize power, or we will be destroyed one at a time.**

> Köstring again returned to our old plan of a so-called "short blow" and demanded that it be executed immediately.

According to Ezhov, the idea of assassinating Stalin and/or other Politburo members originated with the Germans.

> Khoziainov had been made aware of that not only by me but by German intelligence, since during the first meeting after we had established contact between us **Khoziainov transmitted to me a directive of the Germans: to speed up at all costs the carrying out of terrorist acts.**

> Besides that Khoziainov transmitted to me the directives of German intelligence that in connection with my dismissal from work in the NKVD and the naming of Beria as People's Commissar for Internal Affairs **German intelligence considered it essential to assassinate someone among the Politburo members and by this means to provoke a new leadership in the NKVD.**

> In this same period **in the NKVD itself there began arrests of the active members of the conspiracy which I headed,** and then we concluded that **it was essential to organize a mass action on November 7, 1938.** (67)

Ezhov again attributes the plan to assassinate Soviet leaders to the Germans.

> Answer: In the last days of November 1938 I was dismissed from work in the NKVD. Then I finally understood that the Party did not trust me and the moment of my exposure was approaching. I started to seek a way out of the situation I had created and **decided not to stop at anything in order to either carry out the assignment of German intelligence, to kill one of the members of the**

Politburo, or to flee abroad myself and save my skin.

... I told Lazebny: "There is no way out for you, you are going to be destroyed in any case, but by sacrificing yourself you might save a large group of people." When Lazebny questioned me about this **I informed him that the murder of Stalin would save the situation in the country. Lazebny agreed.** (69)

Boris Berman

Pavliukov, who has had access to NKVD documents not cited by others, transmits this testimony concerning Ezhov's conspiracy from Boris D. Berman. It confirms what we know from the other sources we have.

> ...[T]he confessions made by B.D. Berman during the fourth week of January 1939, had dotted almost all the "i's" as concerns the political accusations against Ezhov. Berman, the former chief of the Transportation Directorate of the NKVD and, before that, Commissar of Internal Affairs of Belorussia, declared that unjustified mass arrests, as a result of which completely innocent persons died, were conducted by Ezhov and Frinovsky on the instructions of foreign intelligence services while at the same time actual spies, diversionists and terrorists remained at liberty. By this time Berman had already 'confessed' to contacts with German intelligence, so that such knowledge concerning Ezhov could not compromise himself in any way.

Pavliukov cites the following direct quotation from Berman's statement:

> It was important to both Ezhov and Frinovsky **to create as much damage to the Party and in the country as possible and to strive, through their hostile work in the NKVD, to ruin the authority of the Party, the authority of the Central Committee, as much as possible among the wide**

circles of the population. This was Ezhov's and Frinovsky's principal assignment, and they acted in this direction, involving and corrupting the apparatus of the NKVD both in the periphery and, especially, in the center. **This was done upon the directive of foreign intelligence services of aggressor countries... with whom Ezhov and Frinovsky were tied and whose agents they were.** (Pavliukov, 516-517)

Chapter 13. Ezhov's interrogation of August 4, 1939

Ezhov's interrogation confession of August 4, 1939 is a most important document for understanding the mass repressions. In it Ezhov explains how he carried out the mass repressions of innocent persons and duped Stalin and the Soviet leadership into believing that it was a battle against subversion. Ezhov also touches on this topic in other interrogations, of which only certain sections have been published. We consider them in the next chapter.

Mainstream Soviet historiography ignores this confession-interrogation of Ezhov's. No wonder! For it demonstrates how invalid the "anti-Stalin paradigm" of Soviet history is. We will give lengthy quotations from this document and comment on them. I have put an English translation of the whole text online.[1] Unless otherwise specified, quotations are from this translation.

Ezhov begins by asserting that there was some validity to the charge that returned kulaks, criminals, and others were indeed causing disruption in the country. Therefore the repressions were initially welcomed by the Soviet population.

> Question: Did you achieve your provocational, conspiratorial aims in carrying out these mass operations?
>
> Answer: **The first results of the mass operation were completely unexpected by us conspirators. Not only did they not create dissatisfaction among the population with the punitive policy of Soviet power, but on the contrary they**

---

[1] English translation:
https://msuweb.montclair.edu/~furrg/research/ezhov080439eng.html Russian original:
https://msuweb.montclair.edu/~furrg/research/ezhov080439ru.html Set Text Encoding to Cyrillic (Windows).

resulted in a large political upsurge, especially in the countryside. We observed a great many cases in which the kolkhoz workers themselves came to the UNKVD and the regional sections of the UNKVD with the demand that we arrest one or another fugitive kulak, White Guardist, trader, and so on.

In the towns the levels of robbery, knife-fighting, and hooliganism, from which working-class regions suffered especially, were sharply reduced.

It was completely obvious that the Central Committee of the All-Union Communist Party (Bolshevik) was correct and timely in deciding to carry out these measures. **Despite the provocational measures with which we undertook to carry out the mass operation it met with friendly approval by the working people.** (Ezhov 04.26.1939, 367)

"Approval by the working people" was the opposite of what Ezhov and his men wanted. Ezhov continues by noting how they turned this situation around.

Question: How did you manage to use the working people's sympathy with repression against kulaks, counter-revolutionary clerics, and criminals, in order to attain the goals set by the conspiratorial organization?

Answer: In the provinces, when the so-called "limits" that had been set of the numbers of former kulaks, White Guards, counter-revolutionary clerics, and criminals to be repressed had been exhausted, **we the conspirators and I in particular again set before the government the question of the need to prolong the mass operations and increase the number of those to be repressed.**

As evidence of the need to prolong the mass operations **we alleged that the kolkhozes in the countryside and the factories in the towns had been heavily infested by these elements,** and **stressed the interest and sympathy of the working people of town and country for these measures.**

Question: **Did you succeed in obtaining a government decision to prolong the mass operations?**

Answer: Yes. **We did obtain the decision of the government to prolong the mass operation and to increase the number of those to be repressed.** (367-368)

Here is the reason for the increases in limits that have been widely publicized as showing how "bloodthirsty" Stalin was. Ezhov told him that the working people showed support for these actions. This also shows that disruptions by anti-Soviet forces were far from ended.

"We Were Deceiving the Government"

The interrogator asks Ezhov to specify whether he had deceived the government or, on the contrary, was acting according to the government's wishes.

Question: What did you do, deceive the government?

Answer: **It was unquestionably essential for us to prolong the mass operation and increase the number of persons repressed.**

However, it was necessary to extend the time period for these measures and to set up a real and accurate account so that once we had prepared ourselves, we could strike our blow directly on the most dangerous part, the organizational leadership of the counterrevolutionary elements.

> **The government, understandably, had no conception of our conspiratorial plans** and in the present case proceeded solely on the basis of the necessity to prolong the operation without going into the essence of how it was carried out.
>
> **In this sense, of course, we were deceiving the government in the most blatant manner.** (368)

I cannot find any quotation of this passage by any mainstream historian of the Soviet Union. The reason should be clear: it directly contradicts the anti-Stalin paradigm, the false notion that all of Ezhov's repressions, mass murders, etc., were planned or at least desired by Stalin, and that Ezhov was just "Stalin's loyal executioner."

As Ezhov explains, increases in repression eventually began to seriously alienate large parts of the Soviet population who could not understand what was happening, and how this repression elicited the kind of opposition and protest from the Soviet population that he, Ezhov, aimed at. He then explains how he and his men managed to stifle these protests, especially those from honest NKVD men.

> Question: After you succeeded in prolonging the mass operations, did you achieve the set aims of the conspiratorial organization to cause dissatisfaction among the population with the punitive policy of Soviet power?
>
> Answer: Yes, once we had prolonged the mass operations over many months **we finally succeeded, in a number of areas, in causing incomprehension and dissatisfaction with the punitive policy of Soviet power among specific sectors of the population**. (369)

Ezhov lists the areas where this policy of repression of innocent persons was successful, and says:

> In all of these oblasts there were more gross anti-Soviet acts of repression against people who were

basically innocent, which caused legitimate
dissatisfaction among the working people. (369)

We won't quote or summarize everything Ezhov says about the
repressions. Rather, we'll concentrate on emphasizing a few crucial points. Ezhov says that Leplevskii, in the Ukraine, repressed
persons who were either not politically active or were in fact loyal
to the Soviet government, while letting the dangerous elements go.

In carrying out the mass operation Leplevskii, like
most of the other chiefs of the UNKVDs who were
not conspirators,[2] spread them out over a broad
front while **leaving the most bitter and active of
the organizers from among the kulaks, White
Guardists, Petliurovists, counter-revolutionary
clergy, etc., almost untouched**. At the same time
**he concentrated the whole force of his blow
against the less active elements and in part
among that part of the population that was close
to Soviet power** [i.e. loyal to the Soviet
government]. (370)

Under Uspenskii, who succeeded Leplevskii in the Ukraine, this
same policy was accelerated.

Uspenskii was completely informed about our
conspiratorial plans and I informed him about them
personally. I personally also gave him concrete
assignments concerning this matter. The result was
that Uspenskii **not only continued Leplevskii's
practice of sabotage but increased it
significantly**.

Uspenskii received additional "limits" after my
arrival in the Ukraine and, on my direction, he did
not limit himself only to repression of former
kulaks, clerics, and criminals, but broadened the
category of those subject to repression to include

---

[2] We will return to Ezhov's claim that Leplevskii was not a part of his conspiracy in a later
chapter.

nationalists, former prisoners of war, and others. (370)

Ezhov describes the negative reaction on the part of the Soviet population.

> **All of this caused bewilderment and dissatisfaction among the working people in many regions of the Ukraine.** This dissatisfaction was especially strong in the regions near the border, where there remained families of those who were repressed.

> The NKVD of the USSR and the Procuracy received many warnings about this from the oblasts of the Ukraine. However no one reacted to them in any way. (370)

Ezhov makes it clear that the central government – Stalin – did not learn of this negative reaction:

> These warnings were hidden from the Central Committee of the Party and from the government.

The negative reaction to Ezhov's mass repression of innocent persons was considerable.

> From what Uspenskii said I know that flights through the border posts into Poland increased as a result of the provocational conduct of the mass operations, especially in the border regions of the Ukraine. The families of those repressed began to be expelled from kolkhozes, and in connection with that, robberies, arson, and thefts began. There were even a few examples of terrorist acts against workers of the village soviets and kolkhozes. Not only families of the repressed, but rank-and-file kolkhoz members and even Party members began to write complaints.

> ... Such in general terms were the results of the provocational conduct of the mass operations in the Ukraine.

We were successful in achieving about the same results in Belorussia too. (370)

Ezhov gives more detail in his discussion of the mass repressions in Belorussia:

He [Boris Berman, NKVD chief in Belorussia and originally a Iagoda man] incessantly demanded an increase of "limits" and, following Uspenskii's example, put "nationalists" into the category of persons subject to repression, **carried out completely unfounded arrests, created exactly the same kind of dissatisfaction in the border regions of Belorussia**, and left the families of those repressed where they were.

There were even more warnings sent to the NKVD and the Procuracy concerning dissatisfaction among the population of the border regions of Belorussia than in the Ukraine. **We left all these too without investigating them and hid them from the Central Committee of the Party and the government. ...** In the other oblasts I enumerated in my confession we achieved analogous results and also **succeeded in creating dissatisfaction among certain sectors of the population.** (371)

Ezhov discusses the operation in the Far Eastern Region (FER), the Donbass, and the Central Asian Republics. His discussion of Frinovskii's actions in the Far Eastern Region give some more detail about how the repression was conducted.

Q: But can it be that in June 1938 this operation had still not been completed in the FER?

A: It had already been completed in the FER. However, **we had arranged with Frinovskii that after he had arrived in the Far East he would send a telegram with the request to increase the "limits"** of the numbers of persons to be repressed,

giving as the reason for this measure that the FER was heavily infested with counter-revolutionary elements who remained almost untouched.

Frinovskii did this. He arrived in the FER and after a few days asked that the limits be increased by 15,000 persons, for which he received permission. For the FER with its small population this was a significant figure.

Q: Why did you find it necessary to renew the mass operation in the FER?

A: **We considered it to be the most convenient and most effective form of sabotage, capable of very quickly evoking dissatisfaction among the population.** Since the situation in the FER at that time was rather tense we therefore decided to exacerbate it even further through the provocational prolongation of the mass operation. (373)

Ezhov summarizes Frinovskii's achievements in furthering their conspiracy by sparing the real counterrevolutionaries while repressing the innocent.

According to Frinovskii's words the mass operation prolonged by us came in very handy indeed. He created the impression that he had thoroughly routed the anti-Soviet elements in the FER and in fact was successful in using the mass operation in order to preserve the more leading and active cadre of the counterrevolution and of the conspirators. Frinovskii concentrated the whole blow of the mass operation on those sectors of the population closest to us[3] and on passive, declassed elements and was able on the one hand to stir up legitimate

_____

[3] Evidently Ezhov means "closest to the Soviet government."

dissatisfaction among the population of many areas of the FER, and on the other hand to preserve the organized and active cadre of the counterrevolution. (373-374)

The "Foreign Operations"

The interrogator asked about the so-called "foreign operations."

> Q: Above you have touched on the question that you also utilized the mass operations concerned with the repression of persons of foreign origin from the capitalist countries neighboring with us (refugees, political emigrants, and others) in a provocational manner in the interests of realizing your conspiratorial plans.

Ezhov discusses how the "foreign operation" intended by the Stalin government to rid the country of spies, was turned by himself and his men into another massive repression of innocent Soviet citizens.

> The mass operations concerning the repression of persons of foreign origin from neighboring capitalist countries had as their goal to destroy the base of foreign intelligence services within the USSR. They took place at the same time as the mass operations against kulaks, criminals, et al.
>
> **We conspirators naturally could not carry out these operations without trying to use them for our conspiratorial ends.**
>
> **We conspirators decided to conduct these operations too on a broad front and strike as great a number of persons as possible,** all the more so since there were no definite limits assigned to these operations and, accordingly, we were able to broaden them at will according to our judgment.
>
> Q: What were your aims in carrying out these operations?

A: **The aims** that we pursued in the provocational conduct of these operations **also consisted in causing dissatisfaction and ferment within the Soviet population who belonged to these nationalities.** Besides that **we hoped, by the provocational conduct of these operations, to create the public opinion in European states that people in the USSR are being repressed solely according to the criterion of nationality, and to stimulate protests by some of these states.**

I must say that all this also coincided with **our conspiratorial plans of orienting ourselves towards the seizure of power during wartime,** insofar as it created the prerequisite conditions for this. **These conditions in the present case were expressed in creating a condition of dissatisfaction not just with the punitive but also with the national policies of Soviet power.**

Asked whether this policy of massive repression of innocent persons on national pretexts was successful, Ezhov asserted that it was.

[W]e succeeded in achieving the result that among the Soviet population of nationalities under repression we created a great sense of alarm, incomprehension concerning the purpose of these repressions, dissatisfaction with Soviet power, talk about the approach of war, and a strong orientation towards emigration.

An important result for Ezhov's purposes were the protests of foreign countries and of some well-known individuals.

... as a result of the provocational conduct of these operations there were many protests on the part of the government of Germany, Poland, Persia, Greece, and other states, and articles of protest appeared in a number of newspapers of European countries.

According to Ezhov, Iran, Greece, Finland, England, Germany, Poland, and France protested.

> Besides that, as I have already said, **in the European press a number of articles of protest appeared, which succeeded in evoking incomprehension and protests even among friends of the Soviet Union.**

> Question: And namely?

> Answer: I have in mind in the first place **Romain Rolland.** He sent a special letter in which he asked that he be told whether it were true that repressions against foreigners had begun in the USSR that took place purely on the basis of nationality without regard to their attitude towards the Soviet Union. He explained this request by the fact that a number of protest articles had appeared in the foreign press, and then many prominent figures in Europe had turned to him to ask about this, knowing that he was a friend of the Soviet Union.

> Besides that Romain Rolland had already asked about certain persons under arrest whom he knew personally and whom he recommended because of their sympathy with Soviet power.

Ezhov explained how the "national operations" were used to repress anybody he and his men wanted, not only spies or even just those of a given nationality.

> As I have already said, we had decided to carry out these mass operations on a broad front and **to encompass in the repressions the greatest number of people possible.**

> Our main pressure on the heads of the UNKVDs, whether they were conspirators or not, was precisely along these lines with the aim of **forcing them all the time to expand the operation.**

As a result of this pressure **the practice of repressions without any incriminating evidence whatsoever on the sole basis of one criterion alone, that the person repressed belonged to such-and-such a nationality (Pole, German, Latvian, Greek, etc.), was broadly expanded.**

However, that was not enough. The practice of including Russians, Ukrainians, Byelorussians, et al. in the category of Poles, Finns, Germans, et al., became a rather mass phenomenon, especially in certain oblasts.

Of those who especially distinguished themselves in this manner were the People's Commissars of Internal Affairs of such republics as: the Ukraine, Belorussia, Turkmenia, and the heads of the UNKVDs of such oblasts as the Sverdlovsk, Leningrad, and Moscow.

So for example **Dmitriev, former head of the NKVD of the Sverdlovsk oblast included a great many Ukrainians, Byelorussians, and even Russians under the category of repressed Polish refugees.** In any case **for every arrested Pole there were no fewer than ten Russians, Ukrainians, and Byelorussians.**

There were many cases in which Russians, Ukrainians, and Byelorussians generally were made into Poles with falsified documents.

The practice in Leningrad was the same. **Instead of Finns Zakovskii arrested many native inhabitants of the USSR – Karelians, and "transformed" them into Finns.**

Uspenskii, under the appearance of Poles arrested many Ukrainian Uniates, that is, selected them not on the basis of national origin but according to their religion. **I could multiply many**

times examples of this kind. They are characteristic for the majority of oblasts.

Thereupon Ezhov outlines the impunity he and his henchmen enjoyed by virtue of the special powers of the judicial system.

Question: Was it only the simplified judicial procedure that permitted you to realize your provocational plans?

Answer: Basically, of course, **it permitted us to carry out sabotage with impunity.**

As a result of such an extremely simplified judicial procedure in the oblasts, for example, **the practice of falsifying investigative facts, forgery, and deception was widely developed.**

Ezhov claims that the Procuracy, which was supposed to oversee police actions, did not do so.

The procurors of the oblasts, krais, and republics, and also the Procuracy of the USSR could not have been unaware of such a blatant criminal practice of mass provocational arrests and falsification of investigative facts, since they bore responsibility, together with the NKVD, for the review of such cases.

This inactivity of prosecutorial supervision can only be explained by the fact that **in charge of the Procuracy in many oblasts, krais, and republics were members of various anti-Soviet organizations who often practiced even more widespread provocational repressions among the population.**

Another part of the procurors, those who were not involved in participation in anti-Soviet groupings, simply feared to argue with the heads of the UNKVDs on these questions, all the more so since they did not have any directives on these matters from the center, where all the falsified investigative reports that had been mechanically signed by themselves, i.e. the procurors, went through without any kind of restraint or remarks.

...The Procuracy of the USSR could not, of course, have failed to notice all these perversions.

I explain the behavior of the Procuracy of the USSR and, in particular, of Procuror of the USSR Vyshinskii by that same fear of quarreling with the NKVD and by [the desire] to prove themselves no less "revolutionary" in the sense of conducting mass repressions.

I have come to this conclusion also because **Vyshinskii often spoke to me personally about the tens of thousands of complaints coming in to the Procuracy and to which he was paying no attention.** Likewise, during the whole period of the conduct of the operations I do not recall a single instance of a protest by Vyshinskii concerning the mass operations, while there were instances when he insisted on more severe sentences in relation to some persons or other.

This is the only way I can explain the virtual absence of any procuratorial supervision at all during the mass operations and the absence of any protests from them to the government against the acts of the NKVD.

Ezhov's Use of the GULAG for his Conspiracy

At the end of the interrogation the interrogator raises the question of the role played by the fact that the NKVD also controlled the GULAG, the labor camps where those not sentenced to execution were confined. Ezhov discusses this question briefly.

Question: It is well known that a large number of those persons repressed in all the mass operations were sentenced to terms of imprisonment in the camps.

How is it that you did not fear the exposure of your criminal practices, since you knew that many of these people were convicted on the basis of falsified materials?

Answer: We, and specifically I, had no fears that our criminal machinations might be exposed by those imprisoned in the camps. **All the camps were not only under the command of the NKVD but were also commanded from the GULAG by conspirators. Under these conditions we could always take the appropriate preventative measures.**

Most important, we had our own special consideration when we sent this contingent to the camps.

These considerations and plans were as follows: **when we sent repressed persons to the camps on the basis of materials that had no sufficient basis we planned to use their dissatisfaction during wartime and, in particular, upon our seizure of power.**

In the next chapter we will discuss Ezhov's testimony about the use of the GULAG camps as a component of his conspiracy.

Chapter 14. Other Interrogations of Ezhov

We do not know how many transcripts of interrogations of Ezhov are in existence. The prosecution materials concerning virtually all the important matters of the later 1930s in the USSR are still top-secret, kept in the Presidential Archives of the Russian Federation.

Under Russian law materials are to be declassified after 75 years. If this law were followed, all of the documents concerning the repressions of the 1930s should have been declassified and should now be available to researchers.

However, as of the time of this writing (June 2016) all investigative materials of persons *not* subsequently "rehabilitated" are still being refused to researchers by the FSB, which is the successor to the KGB – MGB – MVD – NKVD. Ezhov has been denied "rehabilitation" so his file, which must be very large, is not open to researchers. We have to work with what is available. I have collected and translated those texts that have been published.

Certain other materials are also being withheld. One example is the transcript of the Tukhachevskii trial of June 11, 1937. All the military men convicted at it have long since been "rehabilitated." But as of early 2016 the FSB claims that the trial transcript is still at the Procuracy, meaning that it is still under investigation. We assume that this is a legal-sounding subterfuge to prevent the transcript of this trial from being made public. From other evidence we know that the trial transcript would provide the strongest possible proof that Tukhachevskii and the other military leaders were guilty and that the conspiracies alleged in the Moscow Trials were also genuine.

I have compiled and translated all the Ezhov interrogations now available from the following "semi-official" sources:

* Briukhanov, Boris Borisovich, and Shoshkov, Evgenii Nikolaevich. *Opravdaniiu ne podlezhit. Ezhov i Ezhovshchina 1936-1938 gg.* Sankt-Peterburg: OOO "Petrovskii Fond" 1998.

* Polianskii, Aleksei. *Ezhov. Istoriia «zheleznogo» stalinskogo narkoma.* Moscow: «Veche», «Aria-AiF», 2001.

* Pavliukov, Aleksei. *Ezhov. Biografiia.* Moscow: Zakharov, 2007.

A few remarks have been taken from Vassilii Soima, *Zapreshchennyi Stalin*, Chast' 1. Moscow: OLMA-PRESS, 2001.

I consider these sources to be "semi-official" since they are quoted unproblematically by all the anticommunist scholars. For the most part these scholars ignore these confessions and what they may imply concerning Ezhov's mass repressions. No one, however, has made any argument that the documents are false.

I have made available online the original Russian text and English translations of all the extant interrogation-confessions of Ezhov's. (Ezhov, Interrogations) Here I examine only those interrogation-confessions that bear directly on the question of the mass repressions and quote only selections from them.

In some cases we are told that we have direct quotations from Ezhov's interrogation-confessions. In other cases the authors have summarized parts of the texts of the interrogations. Usually they have done so without telling us why they have chosen some parts and what they have left out. However, the small part of Ezhov's investigative file now public is enough to give us vital evidence about Ezhov's mass repressions.

Ezhov interrogation of April 18 – 20, 1939

According to Pavliukov this is the first confession in Ezhov's file. The quotations are from pp. 519-520 & n. 481 p. 564. The summary is on pp. 520-521.

Summary of other parts of Ezhov's statement.

> Ezhov started the history of his "fall into sin" in 1921, when he worked in Tartaria and under the influence of anarcho-syndicalist ideas supposedly

joined the local group of the 'Workers' Opposition.'
In the following years, the period of inner-party
discussions of the 1930s, he also supposedly
expressed differences in his political views with the
general line of the party. However, the investigators
showed no interest in digging so deeply into the
garbage-heap of history, and they did not permit
Ezhov to deviate long from the basic theme.

Quotation:

Question: What is the point of this expansive story
about these or those 'political waverings' of yours?
As a long-time agent of foreign intelligence services
you must confess about your direct espionage
work. Talk about that!

Answer: All right, I will go directly to the moment
when my espionage ties were formed.

Pavliukov's summary continues:

Ezhov related that he was drawn into espionage
work by his friend F.M. Konar*, who had long been
a Polish agent. Konar learned political news from
Ezhov and gave them to his bosses in Poland and on
one occasion told Ezhov about this and proposed
that he volunteer to begin working for the Poles.
**Since Ezhov had in fact already become an
informant of Polish intelligence, since he had
transmitted to them via Konar many significant
party and state secrets, he supposedly had no
other choice than to agree with this proposal.**

––––––––––

* F.M. Konar – An assistant Commissar of
Agriculture, he was among those convicted and
executed in March 1933 for sabotage in agriculture
at the height of the serious famine. Konar had also
been a friend of the poet Osip Mandel'shtam,

according to Mandel'shtam's daughter Nadezhda (Memoirs).

———————

The Poles supposedly shared a part of the intelligence received from Ezhov with their allies the Germans, and so after a time an offer of collaboration from the latter was also made.

According to Ezhov **Marshal A.I. Egorov, first assistant Commissar for Defense, acted as the middleman [between Ezhov and the Germans].** He met with Ezhov in the summer of 1937 and told him that **he knew about the latter's ties with the Poles, that he himself was a German spy who on orders from the German authorities had organized a group of conspirators in the Red Army, and that he had been given a directive to establish close working contact between his group and Ezhov.**

Ezhov agreed with this proposal and promised to protect Egorov's men from arrest."

Ezhov interrogation of April 30, 1939

This Ezhov interrogation is taken from Pavliukov 525-6 & n. 489 p. 564. According to Pavliukov p. 526, Ezhov named 66 of his fellow conspirators in this one interrogation.

Summary:

The first stage of the investigation was completed on April 30, 1939. In the course of the interrogation that took place on that day Ezhov told about the method of recruiting his subordinates in the Cheka into the anti-Soviet conspiracy and about **the basic direction of the sabotage work in the NKVD. This sabotage consisted in massive arrests without any basis, falsification of investigative**

materials, forgeries, and reprisals against undesirable elements.

Quotation (Pavliukov 525-6)

> **All this was done in order to cause widespread dissatisfaction in the population with the leadership of the Party and the Soviet government and in that way to create the most favorable base for carrying out our conspiratorial plans.**

Here Ezhov confirms the reason for his mass repressions and executions. This is good evidence that this – Ezhov's conspiracy – and not any initiative by Stalin, was the basic cause of the "Ezhovshchina."

Ezhov interrogation of May 5, 1939

Pavliukov summarizes it on p. 526, with no quotations or notes.

Summary:

> ...at his interrogation of May 5 1939 Ezhov recounted the work of the "conspirators" in the Commissariat of Foreign Affairs. Here at that same time took place the beginning of the large-scale purge (after the removal of M.M. Litvinov, the director of the division of foreign political affairs). Therefore the theme of subversive activity in the Commissariat of Foreign Affairs was especially timely in those days.

> Ezhov stated that **the goal of this activity was the creation of conditions for the victory of Germany and Japan in the inevitable war with the USSR.** Specifically, they undertook attempts to create disagreements between the Chinese government of Chiang Kai-shek and the Soviet authorities, for the purpose, in the last analysis, of facilitating Japanese seizure of the Soviet Far East.

Here Ezhov confirmed that his general goal was the same as that of the Rightists and Trotskyists, as outlined in the Second and Third Moscow Trials.

Ezhov interrogation of June 21, 1939

This is taken from Polianskii pp. 235-238. It is summarized by Pavliukov on p. 527.

> Rodos: If you intend to lie again and make fun of the investigation, then we will not waste our time. I'd prefer to send you back to prison for a week or so to think it over.

These words suggest that Ezhov was not being tortured or indeed subjected to any physical abuse.

Ezhov confirms his espionage work for Germany.

> Ezhov: I admit that **I was connected with Zhukovskii in espionage work for Germany since 1932.** The fact that I tried to conceal that circumstance from the investigation can be explained only by my cowardice, which I showed at the beginning of the investigation when I tried to minimize my personal guilt, and since my espionage link with Zhukovskii concealed **my even earlier ties with German intelligence**, it was hard for me to speak [about them] at the first interrogation.

In the direct quotation below taken from this interrogation Ezhov tells how he arranged for Zhukovskii to be recruited by the Germans on the strength of his (Zhukovskii's) obvious pro-Trotskyist views.

> Not long before Zhukovskii's arrival there arrived at the office of foreign groups, which at that time was also a part of the Raspredotdel of the CC of the Party and was under my supervision, there had arrived materials that characterized Zhukovskii in an extremely negative way. From these materials it

was obvious that Zhukovskii had carried out a number of trade operations that had been unprofitable for the Commissariat of Foreign Trade. **From these materials it was also obvious that in Berlin Zhukovskii was involved with the Trotskyists and spoke in their defense even at official Party gatherings of the Soviet colony** [Soviet citizens residing in Berlin].

Semion Borisovich Zhukovskii did not join the NKVD until October 15, 1936. Before that he was involved in foreign trade, which would have often taken him abroad.

Ezhov considered Zhukovskii's Trotskyist sympathies as qualifying him for recruitment as a spy. This is consistent with what we know about Trotsky's conspiracy with Germany, which Trotsky of course denied.[1]

Ezhov interrogation by Rodos of July 2, 1939

This is taken from Polianskii pp. 252-260.

In this passage Ezhov reveals that he was involved in anti-Party activities long before he was appointed to the NKVD in August 1936.

Ezhov: In my hands at that time was in fact all the work of reassigning of leading cadres. Choosing their activities, punishments, directing them for work abroad. **So I did everything that a saboteur could do in such positions. I directed to leading positions people who were weak in professional, political, and moral sense, people who could ruin production, undermine the fulfillment of the Five-Year Plan.** To compromise the Party. **In the Party Control Commission I managed things so as to cover up and not**

---

[1] See Furr, "Evidence of Leon Trotsky's Collaboration with Germany and Japan. *Cultural Logic* 2009. At http://clogic.eserver.org/2009/Furr.pdf A fuller study of this subject, titled *Trotsky's Conspiracies*, will be published in late 2017.

disclose elements hostile to the Party, and to deprive of Party membership and shut out in every way those who were loyal to the Party. Abroad I tried to send those who would probably become spies or non-returnees.

...

Rodos: What tasks did Mnatsakanov[2] give you? Did you hand over to him secret NKVD information?

Ezhov: He was not interested in secret NKVD information. **In the leadership of the Commissariat on the level of heads of departments and their assistants were Gestapo agents.** Then many of them were exposed, as was Mnatsakanov himself. These agents knew more detailed information than I did. So **I told him about Politburo sessions, CC plenums, conversations with Stalin, Molotov, Kaganovich and other leaders, related to him the contents of secret letters and telegrams of the Central Committee and the Council of People's Commissars.**

It has long been known that documents supposedly coming from the Soviet Politburo made their way during the 1930s to the German government. We don't know whether they came from Mnatsakanov, from one or more other German agents, or whether they were forgeries foisted off on the Germans for profit.[3]

Ezhov interrogation by Rodos of July 9, 1939

From Polianskii pp. 262-268

---

[2] Azarii Airapetovich Mnatsakanov was an employee of the Foreign Division of the NKVD.

[3] See Michal Reiman and Ingmar Sütterlin, "Sowjetische 'Politbüro-Beschlüsse' der Jahre 1931-1937 in staatlichen deutschen Archiven." *Jahrbücher für Geschichte Osteuropas* 37 (1989) 196-216.

This interrogation concerns Ezhov's NKVD conspiracy, of which the mass repressions known as the "Ezhovshchina" or "Great Terror" form an important part.

Question: Tell us how and **when you recruited Uspenskii in the espionage-sabotage organization in the NKVD** that you had created.

Answer: I turned my attention to Uspenskii already at the beginning of 1936.

Question: That was when he was still the assistant commandant of the Moscow Kremlin for internal security?

Answer: Yes.

Q: Where did you find out about Uspenskii's hostile anti-Soviet views. Did he express them to you himself?

A: No. Veinshtok and Frinovskii told me about that. They knew him well and **believed that he'd be very suitable for espionage work.**

Q: Did you recruit Uspenskii personally?

A: Yes. That was right after my arrival in the Commissariat. He quickly agreed and I told him that we needed our own men in the provinces. That was why I sent him to Western Siberia.

Q: What kinds of assignments did you given him then?

A: **He was supposed to recruit agents into our organization from among the Chekist[4] cadre and to promote them to leading positions so that they could seize power in the event of war or a coup.**

---

[4] "Chekist" means NKVD man. The original name for the police organization was "Cheka," an acronym for "Extraordinary Commission" for combating counterrevolution.

Q: In November 1937 you sent Uspenskii a coded message with the following content: "If you think you are going to sit in Orenburg for five years, you are mistaken. Very soon, it seems, I will have to promote you to a more responsible post."

Q: What is the meaning of this message?

A: At that time the leadership of our organization decided to move to active measures. **There was a lot of evidence against Leplevskii and Zakovskii showing that they were spies and enemies of the people.** It was impossible to hide such matters, and we had to get rid of these people, we couldn't use them, they could cause everything to fail. We decided to replace them with Uspenskii and Litvin. I gave Uspenskii a coded message so that **he would find out about his forthcoming departure from Orenburg and would switch all the sabotage-espionage work over to other people whom he had been able to recruit there.**

...

In September of that year [1938] Litvin was in Moscow and used to come to my dacha. **He told me that the arrival of Beria at the NKVD[5] was the beginning of the end and soon we would all be arrested, since the Party was most likely aware about our plot.** And he also said that he would not give himself up alive and that if they unexpectedly recalled him to Moscow he would shoot himself. That's what happened.

Q: Did Shapiro carry out sabotage activity in the Commissariat of Agriculture on your instruction?

---

[5] Lavrentii Pavlovich Beriia was appointed to be Ezhov's second-in-command on August 22, 1938. This was clearly a sign that Stalin and the Politburo no longer entirely trusted Ezhov.

A: Yes, he did. But for a short time only. I decided to take him into the Central Committee, since there I needed people for subversive work.

Q: He knew that you were a German spy?

A: Yes, **I told him that together we would work for German intelligence, so as later to overthrow the government and come to power if there were a war with Germany.**

Ezhov and Liushkov

When NKVD General Genrikh Samoilovich Liushkov, chief of the NKVD in the Far Eastern Region, defected to the Japanese in June 1938 few persons took his statements as anything more than propaganda. The *New York Times* reported with skepticism on his press conferences under Japanese military auspices. However, since Khrushchev's "Secret Speech" Liushkov's accusations against Stalin have fit into the "anti-Stalin paradigm" and so have been accepted as truthful by historians of the USSR.

Liushkov claimed that all the conspiracies alleged in the Moscow Trials and confessions by the defendants were fabrications by Stalin and that no such conspiracies existed. Liushkov also claimed that despite their confessions at the First Moscow Trial of August 1936 Zinoviev and Kamenev had nothing to do with the murder of Sergei Kirov. Indeed Matthew Lenoe, author of a mainstream study of the Kirov murder, accepts these statements by Liushkov as the most important evidence concerning the Kirov murder.

In 1999 American professor Alvin D. Coox published a two-part article in which he revealed that Liushkov had lied at his press conferences. Privately, he had told his Japanese military handlers that in fact there were conspiracies among Party and military leaders in the Far Eastern Region and that the conspirators were linked with the Rights through Aleksei Rykov, one of the major defendants in the Third Moscow Trial of March 1938. Lenoe had simply failed to mention this fact, which disproves his whole thesis about the Kirov murder and, in fact, dismantles much of the "anti-

Stalin paradigm" by itself. We have examined Liushkov's statements to the Japanese in Chapter 17 of *The Murder of Sergei Kirov*.

Coox did not know that Liushkov himself was a conspirator who was guilty of the mass executions of innocent people. In his 2000 doctoral dissertation Steven E. Merritt discussed material from former Soviet archives that revealed something of Liushkov's bloody prints in the mass murders of the Far Eastern Region. (Merritt, Purges, Chapter 8) But that in itself did not suggest that Liushkov was any more than an agent of Stalin. Perhaps, as the anti-Stalin paradigm dictates, it was Stalin who was ordering the mass repressions and that Ezhov was, in the words of Jansen and Petrov, only his "loyal executioner?"

In the present interrogation-confession of July 8, 1939 Ezhov discloses that Liushkov was a member of his, Ezhov's, NKVD conspiracy. Because of its importance we reproduce the whole of this section of Ezhov's statement, still from Polianskii.

> A: **I recruited Liushkov** right after his return from Leningrad from the investigation of Kirov's murder. At that time I was already secretary of the Central Committee and Liushkov knew that I was beginning to oversee the NKVD. Therefore, when I called him to my office and hinted that I had information about his ties with the Petliurovists during the civil war in the Ukraine and other incriminating facts, he was frightened and immediately agreed to work for me as a German-Japanese intelligence man.
>
> Q: Did you really have that kind of information?
>
> A: No, I did not have. I made it all up in order to recruit Liushkov. But I guessed that he was a hostile element with a foul past, and turned out to be correct. **Liushkov agreed to become a spy.**
>
> Q: How did you order Liushkov to flee to the Japanese?
>
> A: Frinovskii often told me that he did not like Liushkov. He was cowardly and could betray us all

at any moment. **Upon our orders he was carrying out important espionage tasks for Japanese intelligence and knew a great deal about our subversive and sabotage work.** Frinovskii said that we had to get rid of him, that means, kill him. And he told me that he would take care of that himself. I decided not to hinder him.

Q: Did Frinovskii say how he wanted to kill Liushkov?

A: No. But I think that he wanted to arrest him first, and then in the inner prison to poison him or put him to death somehow.

Q: What a gang! And who warned Liushkov anyway about the danger?

A: I don't know. But Frinovskii wanted to appoint Gorbach from Novosibirsk to Liushkov's place and recall the latter to Moscow, supposedly for a new job, but in reality to arrest him. Liushkov, most likely, found out that Gorbach was already on route to Khabarovsk, and fled across the border.

It has always been a mystery how Liushkov succeeded in walking unscathed across the heavily-guarded border between the USSR and Japanese-occupied Manchukuo. Logic alone suggests that Liushkov must have had some arrangement with the Japanese. Ezhov's confession confirms this: Liushkov was a Japanese spy and a part of Ezhov's conspiracy. His crossing of the border to the Japanese may have been prearranged with the Japanese border guard.

Ezhov interrogation by Rodos of July 24, 1939

From Polianskii pp. 272-275.

Ezhov: The use of poisons for the purpose of terror against the government was discussed by us, **when our original plan of a *coup d'état* and seizure of power fell apart.**

Q: Tell us about this in more detail.

A: Already in the summer of last year **our organization took the decision to organize a military coup on the 7th of November.**

Q: Who was present at this assembly and where did it take place?

A: It took place at my dacha. Present were Frinovskii, Evdokimov, Dagin, Zhurbenko, Zhukovskii, and Nikolaev-Zhurid. That was, so to speak, the general staff of our subversive organization. Oh, I forgot, Litvin was also there, he was coming to Moscow at that time on official business.

...

Q: What did you discuss there at the dacha?

A: We decided that the interior troops [of the NKVD – GF] that were in Moscow and were under the command of Frinovskii as first assistant to the Commissar would carry out **the coup. As for him, he should prepare a fighting group that would annihilate the members of the government in attendance at the parade.** Then **we decided to confirm a final plan for the coup in September or October and to send around directive to our people in the republics and oblasts' about what they should do on the seventh of November.**

Q: And this meeting took place, who was present at it?

A: There were only three of us: Frinovskii, Zhukovskii, and I. Either the end of September or the beginning of October we met in my office.

Q: And what did you discuss?

A: At that time the possibilities of our organization
had been seriously disrupted by the arrival of Beria
in the NKVD. He replaced Frinovskii, and we could
no longer use the internal troops.

Q: But why, he must have had his agents there?

A: Yes, he did have his agents, but obviously Beria
already had information about our conspiracy and
arrested almost all of them in September. I could
not prevent these arrests or I would have exposed
myself. **Then Frinovskii proposed that we put off
the coup and take power by means of poisoning
the members of the government and in the first
place Stalin, Molotov and Voroshilov. Their
deaths would have immediately caused
confusion in the country and we would have
taken advantage of this and seized power. We
calculated that we could then arrest all the
people in the government and the NKVD who
were unsuitable for us, and to claim that they
were conspirators guilty in the deaths of the
leaders.**

...Frinovskii then said that Dagin would carry out
the poisoning, and that Alekhin and Zhukovskii
would give him the poisons. But it would be
necessary to prepare the poisons, and we decided
to carry out this terrorist act when the requisite
poisons were collected. **We agreed to meet when
Dagin had the poisons and to put together a
detailed plan for the coup.** But Zhukovskii was
unexpectedly arrested, a few days after this
meeting, and after him Alekhin and Dagin, and I do
not know whether or not Dagin received the
poisons.

These three men were indeed all arrested during Ezhov's last
months as head of the NKVD. Ezhov gets the order of their arrests
wrong. According to the information now available Mikhail Ser-

geevich Alekhin was arrested on September 19, 1938; S.B. Zhukovskii on October 23, and Izrail' Iakovlevich Dagin on November 5,
less than 48 hours before the conspirators had planned to strike at
Stalin and the Politburo during the celebration of the twenty-first
anniversary of the Bolshevik Revolution on November 7.

Ezhov and the GULAG

Ezhov interrogation 08.02.39 by Rodos

Polianskii pp. 275-280; Briukhanov & Shoshkov 139-142. Some
text is in both of them.

NKVD means "People's Commissariat of Internal Affairs." Its area
of responsibility went far beyond that of police work and included
labor camps. Ezhov discusses how he and his accomplices utilized
the vast resources of the labor camps and the hundreds of thousands of prisoners in an attempt to further their conspiracy.

> **Sabotage and mismanagement in the
> construction sites flourished with complete
> impunity**. We managed to go over completely to
> questions of defense construction, achieving
> practical control over a significant part of it. **This
> gave us the possibility in case of need in our
> conspiratorial goals to vary and carry out
> different subversive measures which could help
> accomplish the defeat of the USSR in wartime
> and our coming to power.**
>
> ...The greatest population of prisoners was in the
> border regions of the far Eastern borders. Here it
> was very easy for us to take over different
> economic tasks of a defense nature because of the
> lack of workers. However **the camps of the Far
> Eastern Region were situated not only near to
> the borders but we sent there mostly prisoners
> sentenced for espionage, diversion, terror and
> other more serious crimes**, and we sent almost no
> so-called "ordinary" prisoners.

In this way along the borders of the FER, in the direct rear of the Red Army was prepared the most active and embittered counterrevolutionary force, which we planned to use in the widest possible manner in case of complication or of war with the Japanese... A significant quantity of prisoners were concentrated on our western borders of Ukraine, Belorussia, the Leningrad oblast', and the Karelian ASSR, especially in road construction.

... The whole conspiratorial plan of the regime we created for the prisoners consisted in that the most privileged conditions were created for the prisoners sentenced for the most serious crimes (espionage and terrorism), since that was the qualified force that would often be used for directing the administrative and economic work in the camps. In their hands was concentrated also all the cultural and educational work of the prisoners. It is clear in what spirit they were educated. Finally the regime created in the camps often permitted the counterrevolutionary activity of the prisoners to continue with complete impunity.

In the camps the work of the so-called 3rd sections was so badly organized and the camps were guarded so poorly, that **the prisoners had the possibility of creating their own counterrevolutionary groups in the camps and to associate with each other at will. Facts like this were many. The guard of the camps was extremely small, made up of unreliable people, the material situation of the soldiers and the command staff was very poor, and, finally, the prisoners themselves were used in many cases in the capacity of guards. As a result of a security organized like this there were many**

cases of mass escapes from the camps. We fought against this evil poorly and did so consciously, in the hopes that the escapees from the camps would continue their counterrevolutionary activity and would become a force that would spread all kinds of anti-Soviet agitation and rumors. (Briukhanov and Shoshkov 140. The final paragraph above is also in Polianskii 279).

At the beginning of 1937 Frinovskii and I conferred with each other and decided that **we had to have our own man in the Far East, through whom we could maintain contact with Japanese** intelligence. In the event of an attack by the Japanese he was to let the counterrevolutionaries out of the camps, seize with their help the stores of arms and military supplies, and then head terrorist-diversionist work in the rear of the Red Army. We thought about this **and chose Liushkov for these purposes**, whom I had already recruited to our organization in 1936. Then I transferred him from the Azovo-Chernomorskii region and made him the head of the NKVD in the Far Eastern Region.

Q: In which other areas did you create the same kind of espionage-diversionist centers?

A: We also did this **in the western borders of the USSR**. A significant quantity of prisoners were concentrated on our western borders of Ukraine, Belorussia, the Leningrad oblast', and the Karelian ASSR.

Q: In Leningrad oblast and Karelia Litvin was in charge for you, of course?

A: Yes. I sent him there specially at the beginning of 1938 instead of Zakovskii, whom I could not fully trust.

Q: And **in the Ukraine?**

A: **There Uspenskii carried out all the assignments, including contact with Polish and German intelligence.** That is why I made him Commissar of Internal Affairs of the Ukraine.

Ezhov also discussed his use of GULAG prisoners in a face-to-face confrontation (*ochnaia stavka*) with Zhukovskii on July 21, 1939. This is in Polianskii, pp. 269-272; in Briukhanov and Shoshkov, pp. 138-139.

We conspirators had special plans about the GULAG about which I have given detailed confessions, and I decided to bring Zhukovskii up to date. By this time the people who could have exposed **Zhukovskii along the lines of his Trotskyist and espionage connections** were already condemned and the danger of Zhukovskii's arrest had passed. I told Zhukovskii about **the existence of the conspiracy in the NKVD, that the conspiratorial organization is connected with governmental circles of Germany, Poland, and Japan.** I don't remember exactly now, but I think that I told him about our desire to get into contact with the English. Then I told him about the leading members of the conspiratorial organization and about our plans, **specifically about our terrorist plans**...

... The conspiratorial assignments concerning the GULAG that I gave to Zhukovskii consisted in this: **we sent to work the GULAG a very great quantity of compromised people. We could not leave them in the operational work, but we kept them in the GULAG for the purpose of forming a sort of reserve for conspiracies in the case of a coup in the country.** I assigned Zhukovskii to maintain these people, but not to connect himself with them along conspiratorial lines, but to carry out all conspiratorial assignments that came to the GULAG through these people...

There were two variants of our plans. The first variant: in the case of war, when we proposed to carry out the arrests of the members of the government and their physical removal. And the second variant: if there were no war in the immediate future, then to get rid of the leadership of the Party and the government, especially Stalin and Molotov, by carrying out terrorist acts against them.

The "two variants" outlined below by Ezhov are the same as those described by the defendants in the Second Moscow Trial and by the conspirators in the clandestine Zinovievist group that murdered Sergei Kirov in Leningrad on December 1, 1934.

Ezhov interrogation by Rodos of August 3, 1939

Text from Polianskii pp. 280-284.

This is an extended explanation of how Ezhov and his men used the GULAG camps to sabotage the Soviet economy, in conjunction with German and Japanese intelligence.

Q: Name the concrete properties where sabotage was carried out according to your instructions.

A: The construction of the Ukhto-Pechersk road has a decisive meaning for the development of the extraction of coal, oil, and other valuable products, without which the economic development of the Northern region as a whole is impossible. Meanwhile **the construction of this road was retarded by us deliberately and in every way, under various pretexts and the resources allotted to it were spread over a large area of work and did not have any effect.** The retardation

in the construction of the Ukhto-Pechersk railroad
is explained in the main by the lack of a satisfactory
plan, which the Commissariat of Roads and Rails
should present. **The saboteurs in the GULAG and
in the Commissariat of Roads and Rails with our
support organized a never-ending dispute about
the choice of the direction of the roads, which
has been going on for a long time now, and the
planning and even the exploratory works in
many sectors have not been begun to this day.**

Ezhov gives a detailed discussion, which we omit here, of sabotage
activity in Kolyma.

Ezhov also discusses the use of GULAG prisoners as a part of their
conspiracy. The text given here by Polianskii is also in Briukhanov
and Shoshkov, where it is attributed to an August 2, 1939 interrogation of Ezhov.

Q: What subversive, espionage and sabotage
activity did you carry out in the GULAG itself?

A: We understood, that the expansion of the
economic functions of the NKVD must express
themselves in the worsening of our basic operative
work. **We proposed to widely use the system of
camps so as to send there the compromised part
of NKVD workers. There are not only
drunkards, idlers and wastrels. Among them
were people with a Trotskyist past, Rights who
sympathized with Bukharin, and Iagoda's
people.** De-facto they were all recruited by us
since, in sending them to the GULAG, we were
hinting to them that we had evidence against them
that could be investigated at any moment. **In this
manner we created a special reserve of people
read to carry out any conspiratorial task.**

But there were many anti-Soviet elements in the GULAG even without this. The conspiratorial leadership of the GULAG remained, for all practical purposes, unreplaced. At the time of my arrival in the NKVD the GULAG was headed by the conspirator of Iagoda's group Matvei Berman, Boris Berman's older brother. **He had put together a large anti-Soviet group of people who occupied more or less responsible posts in the GULAG. Among these people were a great many Trotskyists, Zinovievists, Rights, and it was easy to attract them to our side after Berman left when the GULAG was headed by Ryzhov, a participant of the conspiracy recruited by me, who was sent to this work on my initiative in order to carry out sabotage assignments.** And after his departure for the Commissariat of Forests, **the GULAG was headed by the conspirator and spy Zhukovskii, who was connected with me and who was at the same time my assistant.**

Accounts of the GULAG agree that conditions in the camps were bad during 1937-1938 and improved immediately upon Beria's taking over the NKVD from Ezhov. Ezhov's account here explains this. This fact also helps to exonerate the Stalin leadership, since it was they who replaced Ezhov with Beria.

> Evgeniia Ginzburg, who was in Iaroslavl' Prison and who saw no newspapers, said that the prisoners could tell when Ezhov fell: The draconian regime in the prisons (frequent solitary confinement and deprivation of all privileges) was relaxed one day. The timing was confirmed a few days later when Beria's name began to appear on official prison notices. (Getty, Origins 189)

Chapter 15: The Testimony of Stanislav Frantsevich Redens

In October 2016 my colleague Vladimir L. Bobrov of Moscow sent me some important materials from the NKVD investigative file of Stanislav F. Redens. From July 1934 to January 1938 Redens headed the directorate of the NKVD (UNKVD) of Moscow oblast'. In November 1935 he was promoted to the rank of Commissar of the State Security, 1st rank. From January 1938 until his arrest in September 1938 Redens was People's Commissar (= minister) of Internal Affairs of the Kazakh SSR.

Redens was one of Ezhov's main co-conspirators, a spy and a mass murderer. His file is available to us only by a historical fluke. As of 2016 the FSB archive in Moscow makes available only the files of persons who have been "rehabilitated." As we shall see Redens confessed to capital crimes. His confessions were confirmed by other of Ezhov's NKVD men, including by Ezhov himself.

But Redens was "rehabilitated" in 1961, on the appeal of his wife Anna S. Allilueva[1] and reportedly at the specific command of Nikita Khrushchev. The "rehabilitation" document, available in his NKVD file, states the following:

> From the rehabilitation determination No. 4n-1304/61 of the Military Collegium of the Supreme Court of the USSR of 16 November 1961 concerning Redens S.F.
>
> p. 373
>
> As the case file establishes REDENS, while working as chief of the UNKVD of Moscow oblast' and Narkom [People's Commissar] of Internal Affairs of

---

[1] Anna Sergeevna Allilueva was the sister of Stalin's second wife Nadezhda S. Allilueva, so Redens was Stalin's brother-in-law.

the Kazakh SSR, carried out baseless arrests of Soviet citizens, used illegal methods of interrogation against arrested persons, and falsified investigation materials, and his actions, as indicated in the conclusion, fall under the article of the Criminal Code concerning responsibility for crimes committed while in office. **However, at the present time it is not expedient to decide this question concerning the classification of these actions of REDENS.**

In 1988 and 1989 Redens' rehabilitation was reviewed by the Procuracy of the USSR and his crimes were reaffirmed. But the legal period for withdrawing his rehabilitation had long elapsed, so Redens' rehabilitation remains in effect.[2]

At this present time, therefore, Redens' file is the only file, of all those of Ezhov's closest henchmen, including Ezhov himself, which is open to researchers. Moreover, it includes materials from the files of other NKVD men, including of Ezhov himself, that bear on Redens' case. For example, it contains the transcript of one face-to-face confrontation, or *ochnaia stavka*, between Redens and Ezhov. Here we only cite a few quotations from this file.[3]

Ezhov's Conspiracy

From the Transcript of the interrogation of the prisoner REDENS Stanislav Frantsevich of 28 May 1939:

...EVDOKIMOV beat the leader of the terrorist group "Promparty" PREDTECHENSKII and demanded that he withdraw his confessions of terror, and **from the group of military conspirators he demanded**

---

[2] RKEB 3, 266-268. This document is available online at http://www.alexanderyakovlev.org/fond/issues-doc/67909

[3] The archival identifiers are as follows: TsA FSB (= Tsentral'nyi Arkhiv FSB) R-24628, T (tom, = volume) 1 or 2 (ЦА ФСБ. Р-24628. Дело по обвинению Редеса С.Ф., Том 1 или Том 2), plus the page numbers (C. = stranitsa, page).

retraction of their confessions about
TUKHACHEVSKII. (1, 291)

EZHOV, with KOSAREV and AGRANOV were sent to
Leningrad in 1934 to oversee the investigation of
the murder of S.M. KIROV and see that it was done
properly. He did not do this and instead of working
he got drunk with ZAKOVSKII. **As a result of
EZHOV'S inactivity LUR'E, ("Emil'"), TROTSKY'S
emissary to the Soviet Union who had been
named in SAFAROV'S confessions, was not
arrested in time. The arrest of LUR'E would
have made possible the discovery of the role of
German intelligence of TROTSKY'S and
ZINOVIEV'S in the murder of S.M. KIROV.** (1, 300)

After that I helped EZHOV and FRINOVSKII to retain
IAGODA'S men in leading positions in the NKVD
despite that fact that IAGODA'S own confessions
named many of them.

Although we had agent reports from our secret
agent ZAFRAN I suppressed these signals and **did
not expose the hostile (literally: "enemy")
activities of the Trotskyist center in Moscow led
by RADEK, I.N. SMIRNOV, KAMENEV and
ZINOVIEV.** (1, 302)

Despite the fact that the arrested group of terrorist
in the field of athletics **admitted their intention to
carry out terrorist acts against leaders of the
Party and government and confessed about
STAROSTIN'S leadership role as an agent of the
Gestapo**, he was not arrested. (1, 303)

For more of what we now know about Trotsky's real conspiratorial activities through his adherents in the USSR see *Trotsky's
'Amalgams'*. We will deal with Trotsky's ties to Germany and Japan
in the next volume, *Trotsky's Conspiracies*.

Volume 2. Concerning the Conspiracy in the NKVD Headed by Ezhov

TRANSCRIPT OF INTERROGATION

of the prisoner REDENS Stanislav Frantsevich

Of 29 July 1939

Question: To what do you confess?

Answer: **I confess that I am guilty of being an active participant in the anti-Soviet conspiratorial organization that existed within the NKVD.**

EZHOV gave me the job of preserving all hostile (literally: "enemy") cadres. He specifically told me that in conducting the investigation not under any conditions to record for myself {*samomu realizovat*} all incriminating conspiratorial materials but to hand them to him personally.... **EZHOV instructed me under no conditions was I to inform the Central Committee of the Party what was going on in the NKVD without his knowledge.**

Question: Was this the extent of your hostile (literally: "enemy") activity?

Answer: Of course not. I carried out hostile (literally: "enemy") work **by keeping safe the conspirators within the NKVD and the Right-Trotskyist underground** in Moscow and Moscow oblast'. (2, 88)

[Redens] EZHOV said to me: "The problem is not to seize power, that is not all, here is what troubles me: What will happen on the day after the *coup d'état*, what will the Party say? What will the Soviet people say? **For the Central Committee of the Party has enormous authority among the Soviet people. So we must patiently undermine the**

authority of the Politburo members. We must prepare everything very well, so everything seems to happen naturally." (2, 93)

Mass repressions

Redens' testimony fully confirms the account of the mass operations that we find in Ezhov's and Frinovskii's statements and interrogations. As Redens stated in the preceding quotation, Ezhov's plan was to undermine the confidence of large sectors of the Soviet population by carrying out massive, violent repression, including mass murder, against innocent Soviet citizens and in the name of the State. This is in fact the phenomenon that anticommunists and Trotskyists call "the great terror."

> Question: What hostile (literally: "enemy") tasks did you carry out at EZHOV'S behest?

> Answer: On EZHOV'S instructions I carried out hostile (literally: "enemy") work in distorting the punitive policy of Soviet power, specifically in the mass operations. **Among the 36 thousand persons condemned in Moscow oblast' were many who were completely innocent.** It was the same in Kazakhstan, where I demanded the intensification of the mass operations. **As a result about 4000 persons were arrested and convicted without sufficient evidence.** (1, 301)

> Answer: EZHOV told me that the main task of the conspiratorial organization within the NKVD that he had set up was to use, in every possible way, the organs of the NKVD of the USSR, by means of the conspirators he had placed around the country, **to overthrow the Party leadership and the Soviet government so that EZHOV could come to power in the USSR.** To further this goal, he had set as one of the primary tasks **the fomenting of dissatisfaction of the population in the country**

and in particular, through myself, in the capital of the USSR – Moscow and Moscow oblast'. (2, 87)

Question: How did you intend to foment the dissatisfaction of the population?

Answer: **By means of the so-called mass operations for carrying out a large number of baseless arrests of Party and Soviet cadres. According to EZHOV these measure would, on the one hand, be directed at the arrest of many completely innocent persons**, and on the other they would help create a great aura of authority for the organs of the NKVD and for EZHOV as its leader. (2, 88)

... EZHOV assigned me to continue in Kazakhstan **to use the mass operations to foment dissatisfaction against the leadership of the Party and the country**. ... in Kazakhstan I did not manage to fully develop my hostile (literally: "enemy") work, although even so **I arrested around 4 thousand people, among whom many people, completely innocent, were shot.** (2, 96)

EZHOV: I told REDENS that it was essential to direct the work of the conspirators in the NKVD, like those in other organizations, in every way **so as to foment the dissatisfaction of the population in the country against the leadership of the Party and the government.** In other words, in the NKVD this meant to carry out **baseless arrests of completely innocent persons.** (2, 112)

The policy of the repression – arrest and shooting – of innocent persons in order to foment dissatisfaction among the Soviet population and direct against the Party and government leadership, is repeated in many other passages in the Redens file. Redens' testimony confirms Ezhov's testimony as we have outlined it in previous chapters.

We conclude this section with one quotation from the face-to-face confrontation, dated August 28, 1939 between Ezhov's assistant Frinovskii, whose confession statement we examined in an earlier chapter, and Aleksei A. Nasedkin, another of Ezhov's NKVD henchmen. Nasedkin was arrested under Beria in December, 1938, and was tried, convicted, and executed in late January, 1940, at the same time as Ezhov and many of his men, including Redens.[4] Apparently this document was inserted into the Redens file because the evidence of these two NKVD men was used in Redens' case. We do not have access to either Frinovskii's or Nasedkin's investigative files, as neither has been "rehabilitated."

> [NASEDKIN]: FRINOVSKII told me that **the conspiratorial organization set as its goal the elimination of the existing leadership of the Party and government** but he failed to say only by what methods he intended to accomplish this. In giving me instructions on practical hostile (literally: "enemy") work FRINOVSKII told me to develop more widely the mass operations and **to compromise the current Party leadership by the arrests of innocent persons.**

Coup d'état and plot to seize power

> Question: When did you intend to carry out your evil plan of a *coup* in our country?

> Answer: Please believe me that I was not informed about all the plans that EZHOV mentioned. For conspiratorial purposes there were many things he did not tell me. Still, **after my frequent questions about this EZHOV told me that he intended to**

---

4 See Petrov, Kto 312 on Nasedkin. Online at
http://www.memo.ru/history/NKVD/kto/biogr/gb344.htm .

carry out this *coup* in either 1938 or 1939. (2, 89-90)

Question to REDENS: Did EZHOV tell you about the goals and tasks of the anti-Soviet conspiratorial organization?

Answer: After I had been recruited EZHOV informed me generally about the goals and tasks of the anti-Soviet conspiratorial organization. **EZHOV told me that the main task of the conspiratorial organization that he had created within the NKVD was the overthrow of the leadership of the Party and the Soviet government so EZHOV'S coming to power in the USSR.** To these goals, EZHOV said, was subordinated all the work of the conspirators whom he had spread around in the apparatus of the NKVD of the USSR. (2, 109)

Question to EZHOV: Do you confirm this?

EZHOV: During the period of my conspiratorial ties with REDENS I fully informed him of the course of the goals set before the conspiratorial organization. **I told REDENS that once a suitable time had been chosen and an essential pretext created for carrying out the *coup* in the country, it would be essential to replace the current leadership of the Party and government and to seize power in our own hands.**

I told REDENS about **the two plans for a possible seizure of power. The first was to schedule the seizure of power at the beginning of a war. The second did not exclude the possibility of seizing power in the country before war, if a suitable moment were to occur.** (2, 110)

[EZHOV]: It should be understood that in these conversations **the plan to seize power by means**

of terrorist acts were always stressed, for without them no *coup* could be carried out. (2, 112)

[EZHOV]: Fifthly, in one of our talks I gave REDENS the assignment of **scrutinizing the people around him for the purpose of bringing them in to carry out terrorist acts against the leadership of the Party and government.** (2, 115)

[EZHOV]: ... I really did intend to use poisons in my terroristic goals against the members of the Politburo of the CC VKP(b). **Specifically, I assigned REDENS to take steps to poison STALIN since I knew that he would be able to carry this out.**[5] (2, 120)

German and Other Foreign Connections

[REDENS]: To this EZHOV added: "As you see, both internal and foreign affairs are now in my hands and the capitalist states will render us full support at the necessary moment, i.e. at the time of the *coup* in the country."

Question: Which states?

Answer: EZHOV was referring to Germany and England. (1, 91)

[REDENS]: EZHOV told me something like this: "Class struggle continues, even though the Trotskyists, Zinovievists, and Rights have been crushed, and the crushing of the conspiratorial organizations in the Red Army is taking place.

None of this happened because the conspirators in the USSR wanted it to happen. In spite of our own will and wishes there is necessity, coercion. Whether this or that conspirator wishes it or not he

---

[5] Presumably because Redens was related by marriage to Stalin and would be able to gain access to him.

must carry out the orders of his real "bosses," who are abroad.

You, REDENS, have one group of bosses and I another. Who these are you do not have to know now; you will know in time."

Question: Stop trying to wiggle out of it. You knew exactly about EZHOV'S "bosses." Why don't you talk directly about them?

Answer: Please believe me when I say that I do not know exactly who EZHOV'S "bosses" are. But I presume that he was connected with either German or English intelligence. (2, 91-92)

[EZHOV]: At last, as my fundamental resources I told REDENS about my ties to the government circles of Germany, Poland, England, and Japan. (2, 112)

[REDENS]: EZHOV told me: "If on the periphery I am more or less at ease, then here at the center it will be more difficult to carry out the *coup*, everything must be well prepared so as not to fail, as it is easy to lose one's head, if you do anything carelessly all will be lost. I have the experience of the failure of the others, I have studied all their mistakes and believe that I'll carry out the matter well to the end, I will not hurry, but I also cannot drag it out too long, because somebody is insisting on speeding up the *coup*.

Question to REDENS: Who, exactly, was insisting upon speeding up the *coup*?

Answer: EZHOV did not say, but it was clear that he was talking about his "bosses" – the leaders of foreign intelligence services.

In other passages Redens makes it clear that Genrikh S. Liushkov, a Iagoda man, was retained by Ezhov Iagoda had named Liushkov in his confessions but Ezhov refused to use these confessions, saying that "Liushkov is ours, " "we trust Liushkov completely," and "we will not let Iagoda compromise Liushkov." On the point of being identified and arrested, Liushkov deserted to the Japanese in June 1938. Liushkov proceeded to claim for propaganda purposes that all the Moscow Trials had been Stalin's fabrications. Meanwhile, he told his Japanese handlers that these conspiracies really did exist. Now we know that Liushkov was an important figure in Ezhov's conspiracy.

Conclusion

The testimony of Redens, Ezhov, and others contained in Redens' investigative file confirms the account of the *Ezhovshchina* documented in the earlier chapters of this book. It constitutes more evidence that the only framework of Soviet history considered "respectable" by mainstream Soviet historiography – what I have called "the anti-Stalin paradigm" – is completely false.

There is no basis to think that all this material was obtained falsely – forged, dictated to helpless prisoners, etc. – and then inserted into various investigative files for some purpose. That is in fact the local stance of those who ignore all this evidence, though they do not have the courage to state it outright.

Chapter 16: Source Criticism of Interrogations and Confessions

In the study of history it is always necessary to base one's conclusions upon primary source evidence. That primary source evidence must be studied and evaluated to assess it for reliability. This is true of all primary sources, including archival documents, memoirs, eyewitness accounts, and of course interrogations and confessions.

Any fact-claim – statement about an event that is presented as being truthful – can be deliberately false, false but not deliberately so (the person making the fact-claim aimed to give a truthful account but was mistaken), or true. This is not only the case with confessions and interrogations, but with fact-claims in all other sources as well, from archival documents to oral accounts that exist only as audio files. It is true about all fact-claims made by all persons at all times.

There is no way to prejudge the degree of truthfulness or falsehood of a fact-claim solely on the basis of what kind of source it is or who produced it. Specifically, it is not the case that fact-claims made by prisoners during interrogation are more likely to be false than fact-claims in other kinds of sources.

All sources must be carefully evaluated. An important method of evaluation is to determine whether the fact-claims made in a given primary source are consistent with fact-claims made in other independent primary sources. Often the degree to which different primary sources are independent of one another is easily determined, though sometimes it is not.

Interrogations and confessions

Much of the evidence available to researchers concerning the causes of the Ezhov mass repressions is in the form of interrogations of persons who have been arrested and are in detention – we

will call them "prisoners" -- and fact-claims made by them of a confessional nature, or "confessions."

In mainstream historiography of the Stalin-era Soviet Union the
accepted practice is to regard all such confessions as "fabrications"
– deliberately false statements dictated in some way or other by
the authorities: the NKVD investigators, their supervisors, the
Commissar of the NKVD himself (Iagoda, Ezhov, Beria), or Stalin.
This is done without any attempt to evaluate the fact-claims made
by the defendant. That is, according to a convention widely practiced in mainstream historiography of the Stalin era, there is no
attempt at source criticism of prisoners' confessions. The fact-
claims they make are simply discounted, ignored.

However, this is not done uniformly, in all cases. Fact-claims made
by prisoners in interrogations or confessions are not ignored
when they can be made to fit smoothly into the anti-Stalin paradigm. An example is the confession statement made by Mikhail
Frinovskii dated April 11, 1939, that we have examined in a previous chapter. When Frinovskii outlined how Ezhov's men fabricated
false confessions, his statement is treated as credible. The following statement of Frinovskii's fits well into the anti-Stalin paradigm
and so is accepted as truthful.

> In my opinion I would speak the truth if I declared,
> in general, that very often the confessions were
> given by the investigators, and not by those under
> investigation. (46)

In the same confession statement Frinovskii testifies that the Moscow Trials defendants were guilty, that the conspiracies to which
they confessed were not fabricated but were true. He testifies that
Bukharin, Rykov, Iagoda, and Bulanov knew that Ezhov was part of
the conspiratorial bloc and did not reveal this at trial. Frinovskii
testified that "Ezhov kept himself aloof" from the preparation of
the Third Moscow Trial – he did not falsify it. These statements by
Frinovskii do not fit the anti-Stalin paradigm. On the contrary: they
dismantle it entirely. These parts of Frinovskii's statement are rou-
tinely ignored.

For example, in the recent (2015) collection by Shearer and Khaustov only the first paragraph of Frinovskii's statement is reproduced – the part where he says that he is going to confess. Nothing at all of his dramatic confession itself is given. No doubt the editors "do not believe" it. (Shearer & Khaustov 236-237)

One of the very few scholars who does at least cite this confession statement of Frinovskii's as evidence is Stephen G. Wheatcroft. In his 2007 essay Wheatcroft, one of the best mainstream historians of the Stalin period, cites Frinovskii's statement in a way that tends to undermine its validity but with no evidence provided. On page 42 Wheatcroft writes:

> According to **Frinovskii's forced statements** taken after his arrest, Yezhov went to pieces at this time.
>
> > Check to see whether Zakovskii and all Yagoda's people have been executed, because after Beria's arrival the investigation of these cases may be renewed and they may turn against us.
>
> Of course there are grave doubts as to how we should treat **these forced depositions,** but they are interesting. Either they were what really happened, or if not, then they were something that Beria's investigators were imagining could have happened. (Wheatcroft, Agency 42)

Wheatcroft completely avoids the issue of source criticism. What does "forced" mean? Are all confessions "forced?" Once you have called the deposition "forced," does that make it invalid? Wheatcroft does not discuss this obviously very important question, as though there were no way to resolve it – that is, no way to attempt to test the usefulness of this document (Frinovskii's confession statement) as evidence.

Moreover, what Wheatcroft says here is vacuous with respect to the possibilities he names: that Frinovskii was telling the truth, or that Beria's investigators "imagined" that this "could have happened." That is, it was either true or false but, if false, made to ap-

pear other than absurd. That could be said about almost any deliberate lie, since lies are normally told in a way that "could be" true.

Wheatcroft concludes:

> It is possible that in this one instance they ["these
> forced depositions"] may be telling us something
> that really happened.

Wheatcroft avoids the issue again. What does "possible" mean
here? Why "in this one instance"? Why not in many instances, or in
no instance at all?

It appears that Wheatcroft does not realize that *in calling
Frinovskii's confession "forced" he is not in fact making a statement
about what Frinovskii said at all*. Rather, he is telling us something
about *himself*, his own attitude. Wheatcroft is really saying: "*It is
my opinion* that Frinovskii's confession was 'forced'."

But the fact that Wheatcroft chooses to regard it as "forced" does
not mean that it is *not* truthful, or is "less likely to be truthful."
Likewise, the fact that some other person does *not* regard
Frinovskii's confession as "forced" does not mean that it *is* truthful,
or more likely to be truthful. In the absence of evidence, as here,
statements such as "the confession was "forced," "the confession
was *not* "forced," are statements about the person who is making
the statement. They say nothing at all about the confession itself.
They are not objective.

When Wheatcroft calls Frinovskii's confession "forced" he is committing the logical fallacy of *petitio principii*, "begging the question." He is "assuming that which must be proven." What we must
do is to assess Frinovskii's statement, and all historical sources,
objectively.

Evaluating confessions made under interrogation

Source criticism is always necessary. It is invalid to *assume* that a
confession is a fabrication just as it is to assume it is what the person under interrogation wanted to say.

We can, and are obligated to, evaluate – verify – interrogations and
confessions in the same way we verify any other evidence. We

check to see if there are any fact-claims that are also made in other documents. If there are, we ask whether they could have been "co-ordinated" so as to look genuine when they were not, or whether such coordination can be ruled out. In the latter case, the fact-claim can be accepted as genuine, meaning: it represents what the speaker wished to say. Sometimes we can assess it as to truthfulness as well.

In all source criticism the student must begin with studying the evidence by reading it carefully and repeatedly. We must attempt to determine the reliability of the testimony by trying to discover whether some of the fact-claims contained in it can be verified in other sources that are independent of it. When two or more independent sources agree on the same fact-claim, the likelihood that that fact-claim is true increases dramatically. If we can verify a number of fact-claims made in these interrogation confessions through independent sources, then we have established that the testimony under study should be considered to be legitimate evidence.

This is the process we have undertaken here. *Every time we can check a statement made in the testimony presented here against independent evidence, we find that the testimony under consideration is verified.* This means that we have no objective basis to reject these confessions.

We have devoted the first twelve chapters of *Trotsky's 'Amalgams'*, more than 250 pages, to source criticism of the testimony given at the three Moscow Trials of August 1936, January 1937, and March 1938. We were able to check a great many fact-claims made by the defendants at those trials against independent evidence. Almost all of them proved to be true.

The few exceptions are especially interesting. In the few cases where we can determine today that a defendant lied, we can prove that he was hiding facts from the prosecution that the defendant did not want the prosecution to know. The defendant lied not to falsely inculpate himself, but to falsely exculpate himself.

This itself is evidence that the confessions are genuine, for why would the NKVD or the prosecution "force" a defendant to lie and successfully hide some crime he had indeed committed?

We are able to prove that the testimony of the defendants at the Moscow Trials was truthful whenever it can be checked. That means that the interrogation-confessions at the Moscow Trials are what they appear to be. They represent what the defendants chose to say, not what they were "forced" to say. The interrogation-confessions of the Moscow Trials defendants are therefore judged to be valid evidence.

Frinovskii's statement of April 11, 1939

In an earlier chapter we studied this important confession statement by Mikhail Frinovskii. Frinovskii confirms what we know from much other, independent evidence: that the conspiracies alleged in the First Moscow Trial against Zinoviev and Kamenev, and in the Third Moscow Trial against Bukharin, Rykov, Iagoda, and others, did in fact exist.

Absent evidence to the contrary, we can accept Frinovskii's account in this statement as falling into one of the latter two categories: either true, or what Frinovskii believed to be true. But Frinovskii's fact-claims demolish the anti-Stalin paradigm! This is why this evidence is ignored by mainstream anticommunist historians: not on objective grounds, but because it does not fit the required, but radically invalid and false, paradigm of Stalin-era Soviet history that dominates the academic study of this period.

Source criticism of Ezhov's interrogation-confessions

Ezhov's interrogation-confessions must be subjected to source criticism using the same method. We must try to check as many fact-claims made by Ezhov as we can against other sources. As in the case of Frinovskii's statement, there are not as many other sources with which to compare Ezhov's fact-claims as there are for the Moscow Trials testimony, a much larger amount of text. Nevertheless, some of Ezhov's fact-claims can be checked against other sources.

Mar'iasin

Lev Efremovich Mar'iasin was Chairman of the directorate the State Bank. Ezhov names him in his interrogation of June 16, 1939:

> Question (Investigator Rodos): Were you friends with Piatakov?
>
> Answer (Ezhov): Never. Mar'iasin, the president of the Gosbank, introduced us. We would get together for a drinking bout sometimes at his place, sometimes at Piatakov's. And then I always got angry with Piatakov.
>
> ...Q: ...When was this?
>
> A: In 1930 or 1931, I can't remember now. (Polianskii, Ezhov 230-233)

Mar'iasin did not become Chairman of the Directorate of the State Bank until 1934. In 1930-1931 he was a member of the Directorate but not its chairman. By 1939, when this interrogation took place, Mar'iasin was dead. He was chairman from 1934 to 1938.

At his trial in February 1940 Ezhov repudiated his confessions and claimed they were all false. But he does confirm this specific fact-claim.

> I have already told the investigation about my enmity with Piatakov. In 1931 Mar'iasin tried to make peace between us, but I refused to do it.

Here Ezhov asks the court to consult the text of one of his confessions in order to find out the truth about his attitude towards Piatakov. Here Ezhov himself verifies a fact-claim that he made in one of his confessions. Ezhov is telling the court: "This statement in that confession of mine is true." But Ezhov has just told the court that his confessions are false! Evidently he did not recognize the contradiction.

Ezhov also confirmed that Mar'iasin had been his friend:

With Mar'iasin I had personal, everyday ties for a long time.

According to Frinovskii Ezhov had ordered Mar'iasin to be beaten repeatedly.

Mar'iasin was arrested, the former chairman of the State Bank, with whom Ezhov had been in close relations before his arrest. Ezhov exhibited an exceptionally great interest in the investigation of his case. He led the investigation on his case personally and was often present at the interrogations. Mar'iasin was held the entire time in the Lefortovo prison. **He was beaten ferociously and continually. If other persons under arrest were beaten only up to the moment they confessed, Mar'iasin was beaten even after the investigation had ended and no more confessions were being taken from him.**

Once, as I walked around the interrogation rooms with Ezhov (and Ezhov was drunk) we dropped in on an interrogation of Mar'iasin and Ezhov spoke for a long time with Mar'iasin, told him that he had still not said everything and, in particular, made a remark to Mar'iasin about terror in general and a terror act against himself, Ezhov, **and then stated that "we will beat, beat, beat you."** (Frinovskii, 46)

In his confession of November 15, 1938, I.N. Dagin, one of Ezhov's "investigator-bonebreakers," testified as follows:

One time, at the end of October or the beginning of November of this year, I stayed in the Kremlin on official business. Knowing that Ezhov was not sleeping (this was about 6 o'clock in the morning) I phoned Ezhov. From his voice I could clearly tell that Ezhov was in a seriously inebriated condition.

> ... Suddenly Ezhov glared at me and said, gritting his teeth and clenching his fist:
>
> "What, you have all led me on? And this Nikolayev, the swine, is giving confessions against everyone... We'll cut him to pieces.
>
> -- I had this good friend, Mar'iasin – continued Ezhov, we worked together in the CC. Mar'iasin opposed our business **and for that he was beaten every day by my order...**
>
> -- Mar'iasin's case was long finished, it had been set to be heard, but **I arranged for it to be postponed each time in order to continue to beat Mar'iasin. I ordered them to cut off his ear, his nose, to poke out his eyes, to cut Mar'iasin into pieces.** And that's the way it's going to be with all those..."
> (Petrov & Iansen, 350)

Both Frinovskii and Dagin testify that Ezhov had Mar'iasin savagely beaten. In his final statement at trial and after having repudiated his confessions Ezhov still admitted that he had had Mar'iasin beaten:

> When he had been arrested, for a long time Mar'iasin did not confess about his espionage and provocations in relation to the members of the Politburo. **That is why I gave the order to "beat up" Mar'iasin.**

Frinovskii and Dagin agree that Ezhov had Mar'iasin badly beaten. Ezhov too agrees. This is another instance where Ezhov, having just declared his confessions to be false, then confirms that the confessions of others about some of his actions are true, and therefore a statement in one of his confessions is true as well.

Ezhov's birth

In his interrogation of October 25, 1939, by NKVD investigator Esaulov, Ezhov claims to clarify the question of his birth.

> Q: In official documents you lied that you were born
> in Petrograd. No information about your birth in
> that city has been found. Where were you born in
> reality?
>
> ...
>
> A: I only know about the place I was born from my
> mother's words, from memories of my early
> childhood. Mother said that I was born in the city of
> Mariampol [today Marijampolé, Lithuania – GF], in
> the former Suval'sk guberniia of Lithuania.
> Afterwards I went to Petrograd. By means of the
> facts about my birth in Petrograd I wanted to
> portray myself in the guise of a deeply-rooted
> proletarian and old revolutionary.

In the confession already cited Dagin confirms Ezhov's confusion
about his place of birth.

> ... Then we all began to review documents that
> Ezhov brought, and during this he made the
> following remark: "Here is everything almost from
> the day of my birth, although where I was born, I
> myself do not know, no one knows. I believe I was
> born in Leningrad, but according to the way my
> mother told it, somewhere on the road, the devil
> knows where."

> ... I seem to remember that sometime earlier Ezhov
> had somehow mumbled to me that he had been
> born of Polish blood, his grandfather or someone
> else was of Polish descent.

Once again, Dagin's confession verifies a fact-claim from one of
Ezhov's confessions.

Liushkov

NKVD General Liushkov was sent to the Far East by Ezhov in 1937
and defected to the Japanese in June 1938. Under Japanese auspices Liushkov gave press conferences in which he claimed that all

the allegations of conspiracies, beginning with the First Moscow Trial of August 1936 (the Zinoviev-Kamenev trial) were fabrications by Stalin. But this was purely for propaganda purposes. Privately, Liushkov gave his Japanese military handlers details about real conspiracies in the Far East among the military commanders and about their ties to the Rights through Rykov. Liushkov confirmed that the conspiracies existed. His testimony, as uncovered by Alvin Coox, dismantles the anti-Stalin paradigm.

But Liushkov did not tell the Japanese, or of course admit at his press conferences, that he himself was part of Ezhov's conspiracy to overthrow Stalin, or that he himself was responsible for mass repressions, including the falsification of evidence. This was revealed by Stephen Merritt's dissertation in 2000. Merritt writes:

> Material from both the testimonies of victims and the interrogations of the NKVD operatives themselves, taken when they were later arrested, bears out the claim that the arrival of Liushkov and his group signalled an increase in the use of physical torture and the wholesale fabrication of evidence. Typical of the statements made by NKVD operatives was that by Dimentman, who was to replace Vizel' as head of the Primorsk NKVD. Dimentman stated that illegal methods had begun in Khabarovsk in 1937, when he arrived with the brigade of Mironov, but that the beating and torture of arrested persons began on a mass order with the arrival of Liushkov. (348)

A.S. Suturin's book on repression in the Soviet Far East, cited by Merritt here, contains testimony by NKVD men arrested and interrogated in 1939 under Beria that attests to the fact that, under Liushkov's leadership, they engaged in beating and fabricating confessions against completely innocent persons.

> On May 31, 1939, Semenov said: "With Liushkov's arrival the investigative staff of the directorate, including I, Semenov, used measures of physical action [torture – GF] against those arrested."

"Chief of the investigative section Malakhov gave
the order to the investigators of the Secret-Political
Section to use measures of physical action against
those arrested. Together with Liushkov there
arrived in the region a brigade of operational
workers (Malakhov, Rysenko). They brought
handcuffs which they kept in the investigative
section. Upon Malakhov's orders I, Semenov, put
handcuffs on the arrested person Ovchinnikov (S.I.
Ovchinnikov was the First Secretary of the Ussurii
obkom of the VKP(b) and a delegate to the XVII
Party Congress)."

Later Semenov stated: "The whole investigative
staff of the directorate took part in the beating of
prisoners after handcuffing them. He personally
used measures of physical action at the
interrogation of the chairman of the Ussurii
province executive committee Mishin, and in the
same way he compiled documents against the
arrested Larin, Lukin, and Bragin..." (Suturin, Delo
249)

Frinovskii claimed that Liushkov was one of Ezhov's men for
whom Ezhov lied and covered up from the Central Committee and
Stalin.

A second fact about which I became aware after I
left the NKVD. Ezhov hid from the CC and from
Stalin confessions that were sent from the Georgian
NKVD on Liushkov and other conspirators at the
time of Liushkov's appointment as chief of the
directorate of the NKVD in the DVK [Far Eastern
Region].

Upon Ezhov's instructions I conducted a
"verification" of these confessions against Liushkov
by means of interrogating Yagoda. The
interrogation was deliberately carried out in such a
way that Yagoda did not confirm these confessions

against Liushkov, at a time when Liushkov had been one of the men closest to him. Liushkov, as is well known, fled abroad. (49)

We have already quoted from Ezhov's interrogation of August 2, 1939, by NKVD investigator Rodos, where Ezhov admits that:

> Q: Did you send Liushkov there specially. What assignments did you give him?
>
> A: At the beginning of 1937 Frinovskii and I conferred with each other and decided that we had to have our own man in the Far East, through whom we could maintain contact with Japanese intelligence. In the event of an attack by the Japanese he was to let the counterrevolutionaries out of the camps, seize with their help the stores of arms and military supplies, and then head terrorist-diversionist work in the rear of the Red Army. We thought about this and chose Liushkov for these purposes, whom I had already recruited to our organization in 1936. Then I transferred him from the Azovo-Chernomorskii region and made him the head of the NKVD in the Far Eastern Region.

The evidence cited by Merritt confirms Ezhov's claim that Liushkov was part of his conspiracy. Liushkov's intense hostility towards Stalin is evident from his press conferences.

Both Frinovskii's statement and Suturin's study confirm a fact-claim made by Ezhov in one of his confessions.

The Military Conspiracy

In an earlier chapter we analyzed Ezhov's confession of April 26, 1939. There he outlines the military conspiracy and its close connections with the German General Staff. The existence of the military conspiracy is confirmed both in the confession by Marshal Tukhachevskii that was published in the early 1990s and then reclassified, and by Marshal Budennyi' report to Marshal Voroshilov two weeks after the trial and executions of Tukhachevskii and his associates.

The military conspiracy is also confirmed at length in Genrikh Liushkov's remarks to his Japanese handlers as uncovered by Alvin Coox. We have outlined and analyzed Liushkov's revelations in detail in *The Murder of Sergei Kirov* and won't repeat all this material here.

Both of these sources confirm Ezhov's testimony about the military conspiracy. Testimony at the Third Moscow Trial also confirms it.

Testimony of Zinaida Glikina

During the interrogation of Ezhov on May 11, 1939 by NKVD man Bogdan Kobulov the investigator raised the question of Ezhov's knowledge of the adulterous affair between Ezhov's wife Elena Solomonovna and the famous Soviet novelist Mikhail Sholokhov.

> Q: What can you tell us about her relations with the writer Sholokhov?
>
> A: I seem to recall that, I think last spring, my wife told me that she had meet Sholokhov, who had come to Moscow and dropped in at the journal "SSSR na stroike." There was nothing surprising in this, Ezhova always tried to meet writers and never missed an opportunity to do so. I was very well informed about this.
>
> Q: Good. And what did you do when you found out about the intimate relations between Ezhova and Sholokhov?
>
> A: I did not know anything about such relations; this is the first time I have heard about them.
>
> Q: Don't lie, Ezhov. In June and August of last year upon your instructions Alekhin arranged to monitor the letter "N" at the phone number of the Hotel "Nationale," where Sholokhov was staying.

Ezhov denied knowing about this affair and beating his wife for it:

> Q: ...you did know that the intimate relations of
> Sholokhov with your wife were recorded. Here,
> take a look at this.

> [Here the investigator reads Kuz'min report of Dec.
> 12 1938, according to Polianskii, 224-5]

> Do you admit that a few days after you received the
> transcript you brought it home and showed the
> document to your wife, and then berated her for
> betraying you?

> A: No such event happened. No one ever gave me
> this transcript of the intimate relations between
> Ezhova and Sholokhov, and in general I never
> showed my wife documents from my work and
> never told her what they contained.

> Q: Of course you can deny this, Ezhov. But we have
> the confessions of Glikina, Ezhova's close friend and
> a German spy, who is now arrested and is under
> investigation. Glikina confesses that Ezhova was
> beaten by you and complained to her and told her
> about everything. Therefore let me remind you that
> lying will not help you!"

By chance we have that part of Glikina's confessions that deals with this incident. It was published by Vitalii Shentalinskii, a ferociously anticommunist and anti-Stalin writer who during the early 1990s had access to certain materials from former Soviet archives, evidently including some investigative materials that have since been reclassified and are no longer available to researchers.

As a small part of this confession, which Shentalinskii claims fills an entire notebook, Glikina wrote:

> After dinner Ezhov noticeably drunk and nervous,
> got up from the table, took some document a few
> pages long out of his briefcase, turned to Khaiutina-
> Ezhova [his wife] and asked: "Did you cohabit with
> Sholokhov?" She denied it, whereupon Ezhov with

bitterness threw it in her face saying, "Take it, read!"

Ezhov told Glikina to read it too. She described it thus: "I understood that this document was a transcript of everything that had happened between Khaiutina-Ezhova and Sholokhov in his hotel room, and that this clandestine recording had been organized at Ezhov's order."

> After this Ezhov finally lost control of himself, ran up to his wife who was standing by the divan and began beating her with his fists on the face, in the chest, and in other parts of her body. Ezhov only stopped when I interfered... (Shentalinskii, Donos 421-422)

Therefore, this part of Glikina's confession confirms the genuineness of the May 11, 1938, interrogation of Ezhov by Kobulov. It is significant that Ezhov lied to Kobulov, whereupon the latter had the transcript of Glikina's testimony to confront him. Nothing of the kind would be necessary if the NKVD intended to beat, torture, or otherwise compel Ezhov to say what they wanted him to say.

Therefore these two passages are evidence that, although Ezhov lied for some reason, *the investigation was genuine.* Ezhov was not beaten into a false confession. Nor was he beaten in order to get him to tell the truth – in this case, about his knowledge of his wife's adultery with Sholokhov and his beating her.

On the contrary: the investigator utilized a conventional interrogational technique familiar to investigators everywhere: to try to get the prisoner to tell the truth by confronting him with the testimony of others who have already named him. This is strong evidence that the investigation of Ezhov did not proceed by beating him.

We note in passing that Glikina also confirms Ezhov's guilt in "anti-party activity." Glikina lived with the Ezhovs and spent a great deal of time with them. In the very short passage from her confession quoted by Shentalinskii she concedes:

... However, I do not intend to present myself as completely innocent. I admit that I am guilty in that, **though I knew all about Ezhov's anti-party activities I hid everything I knew** and did not report it to anyone because of my close relationship with his wife N.I. Ezhova and to him personally, and was completely devoted to them. (Shentalinskii, Donos 418)

Confessions of Izrail' Moiseevich Leplevskii

In a passage we have already quoted in an earlier chapter Frinovskii identified Leplevskii as one of Ezhov's "investigator-bonebreakers":

"Investigator-bonebreakers" were chosen basically from among the conspirators or persons who were compromised. They had unsupervised recourse to beating arrested persons and in a very short time obtained "confessions" and knew how to write up transcripts in a grammatical and elegant fashion.

In this category belong: Nikolayev, Agas, Ushakov, Listengurt, Evgen'ev, Zhupakhin, Minaev, Davydov, Al'tman, Geiman, Litvin, **Leplevskii,** Karelin, Kerzon, Iamnitskii, and others. (45)

During his interrogation by NKVD man Rodos of July 8, 1939, Ezhov testified:

At that time the leadership of our organization decided to move to active measures. There was a lot of evidence against Leplevskii and Zakovskii showing that they were spies and enemies of the people. It was impossible to hide such matters, and we had to get rid of these people, we couldn't use them, they could cause everything to fail. We decided to replace them with Uspenskii and Litvin.

Leonid Naumov reproduces a summary report on Leplevskii made in June 1956. This was a period when, by Khrushchev's order, many files of those executed for treason during the 1930s were being reviewed. The report in question is a summary of Leplevskii's file. The report states in part:

> **Leplevskii confesses that when he worked in the Ukraine he did not struggle against the organized counterrevolution but only exposed those whom, given the existing situation, it was impossible to hide any longer** (Liubchenko, Khvylia, Poraiko). At the same time **in organizing the mass operations he would consciously arrest innocent, honest Soviet citizens** so as to be able to show large number and a determined struggle against counterrevolution. **(In the guise of liquidating the Polish underground more than 30 thousand persons were arrested, but the serious counterrevolutionary Polish formations remained untouched.)**
>
> ... From Kosior Leplevskii knew that despite the losses suffered by the conspiracy significant forces of the plot remained untouched, **but in order to carry out a *coup d'état* successfully it was essential to have an orientation abroad towards the Germans and Poles, who were ready to cooperate on this question.** (Naumov, Stalin 541-2)

Leplevskii does *not* mention Ezhov as a leader of the conspiracy. This is consistent with what Ezhov himself testified in his August 8, 1939, interrogation.

> Question: Give more detailed information about each oblast separately, and report to the investigation those facts known to you about provocational methods of repression that were deliberately carried out.
>
> Answer: I'll begin with the Ukraine. **The People's Commissariat of Internal Affairs of the UkSSR was headed at the beginning by Leplevskii, a**

member of the anti-Soviet organization of Rightists, and then by Uspenskii, a conspirator whom I had recruited. The mass operation had been begun under Leplevskii, but Uspenskii's share of repressed persons was no smaller.

Question: **Was Leplevskii aware of your conspiratorial plans?**

Answer: **No, Leplevskii could hardly have known about our real conspiratorial plans.** In any case I myself did not recruit him to our conspiratorial organization and did not inform him of our plan to conduct the operation in a provocational manner. None of the leading conspirators told me that he was connected to Leplevskii in the conspiracy. (369)

Ezhov then describes Leplevskii's activity in suppressing honest Soviet citizens while leaving the real conspirators alone.

In carrying out the mass operation Leplevskii, like most of the other chiefs of the UNKVDs who were not conspirators, spread them out over a broad front **while leaving the most bitter and active of the organizers from among the kulaks, White Guardists, Petliurovists, counter-revolutionary clergy, etc., almost untouched**. At the same time **he concentrated the whole force of his blow against the less active elements and in part among that part of the population that was close to Soviet power**. (370)

The 1956 review reports that Leplevskii fully confessed his guilt at trial. Let's consider this interesting question:

* If Leplevskii had said that he was part of Ezhov's conspiracy, then we could conclude that Ezhov was lying, as he lied about knowing about his wife's infidelity with Sholokhov.

* If Leplevskii had not confessed he might have done so because he thought his best tactic was to deny his crimes or because he was in fact innocent.

In fact the two Ezhov confessions and the 1956 report on Leplevskii mutually confirm each other.

Agnessa Mironova-Korol'

In his book *Stalin i NKVD* historian Leonid Naumov writes:

> Interestingly, in January 1939, S. Mironov-Korol' [S.N. Mironov's full name] was arrested, and almost immediately testified that **in July 1937 in a private conversation Frinovskii told him of Ezhov's intention to come to power on the basis of their group in the NKVD** . Of course, one might attribute this to the imagination of Beria's investigators. But here's an interesting detail. **Mironov's wife Agnes Mironov in her memoirs says almost the same thing: "We thought that Ezhov had risen even higher than Stalin."** These thoughts, according to the text of memoirs, are from sometime in mid-1938. But who is this "we" who were thinking such thoughts? Judging by the text of Mironova's memoirs, she was then talking only with the members of her family, with Mironov's brother, the intelligence official David Korol' and his family, and with the Frinovskii family. (263)[1]

Mironova-Korol' did not in fact know much of NKVD work apart from rumors. But this reflects what she thought, based on her personal contacts. She also reports that even the Politburo members were afraid of Ezhov, or at least wary around him, and that she witnessed this herself. Her testimony is consistent with her husband Mironov's account of what Frinovskii had said to him. And

---

[1] The autobiography of Agnessa Mironova-Korol' is available at the Russian online journal *Pseudology*. This passage is from Part 2 Page 25. See http://www.pseudology.org/GULAG/Agnessa/06.htm It is also at http://www.memo.ru/history/agnessa/Chapt1h.htm

that is consistent with what Frinovskii testified in his statement of April 11, 1939, to Beria, which we studied in a previous chapter.

Ezhov's renunciation of his confessions and his final statement at his trial

Pavliukov describes the conclusion of the investigation of Ezhov's case as follows:

> The last interrogation took place on January 31 [1940], and on the very next day the assistant chief of the investigative section of the NKVD of the USSR A.A. Esaulov composed a protocol of the conclusion of the investigation. Ezhov was given for his perusal 12 volumes of his criminal case. He read through it and declared that he confirmed all the confessions given by him at the preliminary investigation, and that he had no additions to make. (529)

But the next day, according to Pavliukov, Ezhov received a visit from Lavrentii Beria during which he informed Beria that he would now deny everything, that all the charges against him were a complete invention.

What was going on here? Pavliukov makes the following surmise:

> Evidently Ezhov, having understood that after the formal court procedure he would have no chance of remaining alive, had decided to delay the trial, hoping that they would not bring to trial a defendant who had renounced his confessions. And any delay in such an important case might attract the attention of Stalin who, having learned what was happening, might send some representative to find out what was happening. And then at last there might be a chance to tell the Vozhd' [leader, i.e. Stalin] the truth about why and how his faithful pupil and comrade-in-arms had been forced to slander himself.

However, Ezhov's plans – if such they were – were
not successful. (530)

A transcript of Ezhov's trial must still exist. Pavliukov evidently
had privileged access to it or to a summary of it. Evidently it is still
classified despite the expiration of more than 75 years.

Pavliukov describes the trial itself as follows:

> Then the protocol concerning the conclusion of the
> investigation was announced, in which Ezhov had
> confirmed the truth of his confessions with his own
> signature. Ezhov stated that at that moment he had
> not retracted these confessions, but that he was
> retracting them now. He had no connections with
> any intelligence services, had not planned any
> terrorist act on Red Square on November 7, 1938,
> and had never taken part in any conspiratorial
> activity.
>
> It was necessary for the court to set aside its
> preliminary intention to do without witnesses and
> to call into the courtroom one of them, Ezhov's
> former assistant M. P. Frinovskii. That same day he
> too was supposed to appear in court and probably
> was somewhere nearby.
>
> Frinovskii stated that soon after his appointment as
> Commissar of Internal Affairs **Ezhov had recruited
> him into the conspiratorial organization in the
> NKVD organized by himself**. At first they
> prevented the exposure of the participants of the
> Right-Trotskyite bloc as much as possible, and at
> the end of 1937 they set to the creation of a
> terrorist group within the NKVD.
>
> Besides that Frinovskii discussed the falsification,
> in accordance with Ezhov's directives, of the so-
> called mercury poisoning, the murder on Ezhov's
> order of the chief of the Foreign Division of the

GUGB of the NKVD A. A. Slutskii, and of the
poisoning by Ezhov of his own [Ezhov's] wife.

In answer to the questions of the chairman V.V.
Ul'rikh Ezhov called everything Frinovskii said to
be vicious slander. He did not poison his wife and
did not send her luminal, and in relation to Slutskii
had had a directive from "directive organs" not to
arrest him but to get rid of him by another means,
"as otherwise our whole foreign intelligence service
would have fled." The need to get rid of Slutskii was
dictated, in Ezhov's words, by the fact that there
were very weighty confessions of the former
assistant commissar for internal affairs Ia. S.
Agranov.

Ezhov continued that he did not take part in the
anti-Soviet conspiracy together with Frinovskii.
Evdokimov, Dagin, and the other persons whom he
had named in his confessions as participants in the
conspiracy were in fact not such, or in any case he
did not know anything about that. (531-532)

A text has been published that purports to be Ezhov's final speech
at his trial. I have translated it and put it online. (Ezhov, Last)
Briukhanov and Shoshkov make the following comments on
Ezhov's last words:

Reading "the Last Word" it is impossible not to
notice that Ezhov said nothing about the essence of
the accusations leveled against him. He rejected
them all, but spoke mainly about his services in
exposing "enemies and spies of various types and
intelligence services" **while stating at the same
time he had "such crimes for which I could be
shot,"** promising to discuss them, but admitted guilt
only in that he "did not purge enough" enemies.

Ezhov denied his participation in a secret organization directed against the Party and the government, saying that, on the contrary, he had taken all measures to expose the conspirators who had murdered S.M. Kirov. **But was there a conspiracy in the organs of the NKVD? Or did those 14 thousand NKVD men whom Ezhov purged act individually – each one on his own?**

Judging from the transcript [of Ezhov's trial] such a question was not raised at the trial: Everything was clear to the court as it was. The "sincere confessions" in his "Last word" did not ring true. Ezhov was careful to avoid any sharp corners. He even distorted the episode that had already figured in the trial of Bukharin, Rykov and the others, concerning the falsification of a terrorist act against himself. As it turned out the "terrorist act" was planned and executed – if we can even use that word in this case – by Ezhov and by the former chief of the counter-revolutionary section Nikolaev in order to increase the authority of the "iron commissar." Having consulted with specialists about the conditions for mercury poisoning Nikolaev had rubbed mercury into the upholstery of the soft furniture in Ezhov's office and submitted a piece of cloth for laboratory analysis. In the "terrorist act" they blamed NKVD man Savolainen, on whom a vial of mercury was planted. After the necessary "working over" Savolainen confessed to everything.

And Ezhov's attempt to deny the accusation about dissolution in his morals and private life, to convince the court that he was supposedly loved for his modesty and honesty, seems altogether senseless.

> As a whole the "Last word" creates an impression of
> something not thought through, rambling,
> incomplete, and dishonest. And yet Ezhov, in
> essence, had nothing to lose. He could have spoken
> more frankly. (153)

The last two sentences suggest that Briukhanov and Shoshkov believe that Ezhov had only acted upon Stalin's orders. If that had been so then Ezhov would indeed have been a fool not to "speak more frankly."

But we know that it is not true. Ezhov could *renounce* his many confessions. But he could not *refute* them. For one thing the investigators had interrogated those whom Ezhov had named in his confessions, and compared and collated the confessions. Also, the court had the testimony of many others, and witnesses at hand to testify – not only Frinovskii but others, perhaps many others.

Pavliukov did not state the matter as plainly as he should have done. Given the voluminous confessions he had made, and the immense amount of testimony against him, the only thing Ezhov could possibly gain by renouncing his own confessions was to force the court to convict him on the testimony of witnesses. That is in fact what happened.

As Nikolai Bukharin stated at his own trial in March 1938:

> The confession of the accused is not essential.
> (1938 Trial, 778)

This is indeed a feeble attempt at justifying oneself. Very few of the specific crimes to which Ezhov had confessed are mentioned. Nor does a last-minute retraction of confessions that the defendant has just finished affirming carry any conviction. Even a person totally unfamiliar with the facts of the case would ask: Was he lying then? Or is he lying now? On top of which Ezhov admits, cryptically, that he had committed "such crimes for which I should be shot." Such a statement, lacking almost all specifics, calls into question not so much the confessions but the credibility of the person who makes it.

* * * * *

Pavliukov tells the story about how in the 1990s Ezhov's daughter Natalia Khaiutina petitioned to have her father "rehabilitated." In 1998 the office of the Main Military Procuracy determined that there was no evidence that Ezhov had been a traitor (had conspired with Germany or Poland). But it did conclude the following:

> The evidence gathered in this case confirm the guilt
> of Ezhov N.I. in organizing political repression
> against innocent citizens, illegal arrests, using
> physical means of compulsion against those under
> investigation, falsification of materials in criminal
> cases, all of which had irreversible consequences,
> which materially furthered the weakening of the
> power of the State. That is, he was guilty of acts
> aimed at undermining and weakening the state and
> damage to its economic and military power. (545)

Without saying so in so many words the Procuracy declared that Ezhov was indeed guilty of mass repressions. However, it said nothing about *why* Ezhov did these things: nothing about any conspiracy. About treason – the charges of collaboration with the Germans and Japanese and conspiring to overthrow the government lead revolts against it, and murder Stalin and other leaders -- nothing at all was said.

Conclusion

Whenever we are able to double-check a fact-claim made concerning Ezhov's interrogation-confessions or Frinovskii's statement, we find that those documents are true. This is so even in the case where Ezhov was evidently lying in saying that he had not known of his wife's affair with Sholokhov. Therefore, we have no reason not to use Frinovskii's and Ezhov's statements and confessions as truthful

Chapter 17: What Really Happened

In the dominant model of Soviet history of the 1930s the conspiracies alleged by the Stalin government were all bogus. The conspiracy that led to Kirov's murder, the conspiracies to which the defendants in the three Moscow Trials confessed, the Tukhachevskii Affair military conspiracy – all these never existed. All were frame-ups of innocent persons, and all are attributed to Stalin. Naturally, Ezhov's conspiracy never existed either. Michael Ellman believes that the "Ezhovshchina" should be called the "Stalinshchina" since, he claims, Stalin planned it all, Ezhov having been merely a tool. Many conventional or "mainstream" anticommunist historians contend that the "Great Terror" began as early as 1936, or even 1934.

This is not history. Rather, it is deduction from firmly entrenched but demonstrably false premises. If one believes *a priori*, in thrall to the anti-Stalin paradigm, that none of the alleged conspiracies existed, it follows that all were fabrications by the Soviet NKVD and prosecution. If one believes *a priori* that Stalin was an all-powerful "dictator" it follows that everything that happened must have happened because Stalin wanted it to happen. Likewise, the mass repressions must have stopped only when Stalin decided they were no longer needed and it could possibly become dangerous for them to continue.

This whole line of thinking is based on a paradigm that flies in the face of an objective assessment of the available evidence. It represents the triumph of anticommunist ideology over objectivity and is contradicted by all the evidence. We have an immense amount of evidence about each of these conspiracies. We know that Stalin was not a dictator and frequently could not get what he wanted, contested elections to the soviets being the clearest example in our discussion.

In hewing to what we have called the "anti-Stalin paradigm" mainstream Soviet historiography follows political, anticommunist imperatives. Demonizing the Soviet Union serves the propaganda function which remains the primary function of the field of Soviet history as it has always been.

Historians are supposed to be objective, to question their own preconceived ideas and the paradigms that inform those ideas, shape them into explanatory narratives; to give a more generous reading to evidence that contradicts their preconceived ideas and read with an especially skeptical attitude that evidence that seems to reinforce their own biases. If a historian does not begin his/her research with determination to be objective, to discover the truth according to the best evidence and logical induction from this evidence, then that historian has no chance of stumbling across the truth by accident and what he or she does "discover" will not be the truth.

This is why mainstream historians of the so-called "great terror" have failed to attain an account of these mass repressions that fits the evidence. Mainstream historiography has chosen not to do so.

What Did Happen?

The evidence now available suggests that the repressions of the period 1934-1938 saw the following political developments in the Bolshevik Party.

1. The gradual discovering of a wide-ranging conspiracy among many leading Bolsheviks against the Stalin government. These conspiracies developed out of the factional disputes of the post-Revolution period and became particularly acute during the 1920s. After the defeat of the United Opposition in 1927, with the ensuing expulsion and then "capitulation" of most of its members, and Leon Trotsky's expulsion from the USSR in February 1929, the opposition factions, which already had a clandestine, underground existence, endured a period of disorganization.

They were regathered in 1931-1932 as a "bloc" of Zinovievists, Trotskyist, Rights, and other oppositionists. This bloc – all parties, including both its participants and the Soviet prosecution, used this term – first planned to come to power when the Soviet government collapsed under the strain of rapid industrialization and opposition to collectivization, or when the Stalin government failed to cope with an attack by capitalist powers.

During 1933 it became clear to the bloc leaders that the Stalin government had come through the crisis successfully and would not collapse, while capitalist powers failed to invade. The bloc then turned to the tactic of a *coup d'état* and assassination of the Stalin leadership as the only way to seize power. Contact was made, and agreements reached, with at least Germany and Japan, and also with England and France, to gain recognition once their coup had succeeded.

This plan began to be put into operation on December 1, 1934, with the murder of Sergei Mironovich Kirov, First Secretary of the Bolshevik Party in Leningrad, who was assassinated by a clandestine Zinovievist group. Other groups within the bloc such as the Rights and Trotskyists knew that this assassination attempt was being planned and were either planning their own attempt or had agreed not to interfere. The Zinovievist assassin Leonid Nikolaev was supposed to commit suicide immediately after killing Kirov. His suicide attempt failed and he was captured and interrogated.

Because he had no "cover story" prepared – he was not supposed to survive – his attempts to concoct a story on the spot were full of contradictions. The NKVD investigators kept Nikolaev talking. Within a few days, he had named a number of his associates, who were arrested and interrogated in turn. Very soon the investigators had enough testimony to convict the fourteen members of the Leningrad Zinovievist group, and to prove that Zinoviev, Kamenev, and a few of their associates, all in Moscow, were aware of the Leningrad group. The NKVD did not prove that Zinoviev and Kamenev were complicit in Kirov's murder, but only because Genrikh Iagoda, the chief of the NKVD, was himself involved in the conspiracy. However, they and some of their associates were convicted of failing to report the Leningrad group and merely sentenced to prison terms.

During 1935 a conspiracy within the Kremlin library was uncovered. This led to additional suspicions against Zinoviev and Kamenev, since some of the latter's relatives were involved. It also led to suspicions against Avel' Enukidze, who was responsible for the library staff.

In early 1936 the investigation of the Kirov murder was resumed, resulting in more arrests and some confessions. By July there was enough information from these confessions to infer the existence of a much broader conspiracy involving Zinovievists and Trotsky-ists. In late July Zinoviev and Kamenev, confronted and accused by some of their followers, confessed to being directly involved in Ki-rov's murder. This resulted in the First Moscow Trial of August 1936. Defendants at that trial identified others who comprised a spare, or "parallel," leadership group, including Karl Radek, Iurii Piatakov, and Grigory Sokol'nikov. Bukharin and Rykov were also named. On September 26, 1936 Genrikh Iagoda was removed as chief of the NKVD and replaced by Nikolai Ezhov. The Second Mos-cow Trial of January 1937 led to the executions of most of the de-fendants, including Piatakov, and prison for others.

Meanwhile Bukharin and Rykov, as leaders of the Rights, were ac-cused by many of their former supporters. The evidence against them was the first item of business at the February-March 1937 Central Committee Plenum. After three days of discussions and accusations Bukharin and Rykov were arrested and imprisoned.

Stalin had been planning a redraft of the Soviet Constitution since at least 1935. In March 1936 he gave an interview to US news-paper magnate Roy Howard in which Stalin – over-optimistically equating his view with the outcome of the CC vote -- promised contested elections for the legislative bodies, the soviets. The Con-stitution was drafted and adopted in 1936. But at the February-March 1937 CC Plenum there was much opposition to it from the CC members. Most of those who spoke warned against hostility among the population and about anticommunist groups, including returned kulaks, religious figures, former White Guardists, and members of the now illegal Social-Revolutionary Party.

It was clear that most CC members did not want contested elec-tions under these circumstances. Stalin and his supporters argued the case for contested elections but clearly did not convince many, if any. This is not to argue for either side of this debate, since both had valid reasons for their respective positions. Rather, it is to emphasize that Stalin's leadership was just that – leadership. Stalin did not possess dictatorial powers.[1]

On March 1, 1937 Genrikh Iagoda was arrested. He had been implicated by testimony at the Second Moscow Trial and, evidently, by testimony of others under interrogation. By April 1937 Iagoda had begun to outline his own involvement in the Rightist conspiracy and his prior knowledge of the plan to murder Kirov.

In April and May 1937 NKVD investigators had gotten enough testimony from military men involved in the conspiracies already uncovered to arrest some of the leading military commanders, including Marshal Mikhail N. Tukhachevskii. When investigators came to interrogate Ian Gamarnik, head of the Political Directorate of the Red Army, he committed suicide. In late May and early June Tukhachevskii and others confessed to conspiring with the Rights, with the Trotskyists and directly with Trotsky, and with the German General Staff in a plot to overthrow the Stalin government, seize power, and become an ally with Nazi Germany. On June 11-12 Tukhachevskii and seven others were tried, confessed at trial, were convicted, and executed.

During the first week of May 1937 the "May Days" revolt broke out in Barcelona, Spain. Among its leaders were longtime Trotskyists. At the Second Moscow Trial in January, 1937 Karl Radek had called upon the Trotskyists in Spain to stop their plotting against the Spanish Republic or face the consequences. The NKVD had obtained intelligence that German and Francoist agents had been attempting to provoke just such a revolt. At a talk to military officers in early June Stalin said that the Tukhachevskii defendants wanted to make of the Soviet Union "another Spain" – to stab it in the back when it was attacked by fascist powers.

---

[1] See Stephen G. Wheatcroft, "From Team-Stalin to Degenerate Tyranny." In E.A. Rees, ed., *The Nature of Stalin's Dictatorship. The Politburo, 1924-1953*. Basingstoke: Palgrave Macmillan, 2004, 79-107. Wheatcroft argues that Stalin was no dictator up to the early 1940s. Wheatcroft cites no evidence for his claim in the title that Stalin became a "tyrant" or dictator during his last years.

From April 1937 on we have a number of interrogations of high-ranking Bolshevik government and Party officials in which they confess to being a part of the Rightist conspiracy. On June 2, 1937, Bukharin broke his silence and began to give very dramatic confessions of his own guilt in this same Rightist conspiracy.

During the June 1937 CC Plenum 15 members of the CC and 16 candidate members were removed from the CC. Earlier in 1937 5 members and 5 candidate members had been expelled, for a total of 20 members and 21 candidate members since the beginning of 1937. During the rest of 1938 18 more members and 15 more candidate members were expelled. In total, 38 members and 36 candidate members were expelled from the Central Committee. As far as we can tell – little information has been released about some of them – all were expelled for being a part of the clandestine conspiracy of the Right-Trotskyist bloc.

By the time the June 1937 Plenum ended both the Right-Trotskyist conspiracy and the military conspiracy, which was linked to it, were on the defensive. Ten more CC members were removed from the CC in December 1937 and two more in early 1938 for a total of 50. The Third Moscow Trial of March 1937 Right-Trotskyist Trial of which Bukharin, Rykov, Iagoda, and Khristian Rakovskii are perhaps the best known defendants, was the culmination in the demolition of the conspiracy of the bloc.

Elections

A day before the October 1937 CC Plenum began Stalin and the Politburo withdrew their efforts to force competitive elections, required under the new 1936 Constitution. It is possible that the remaining CC members along with the NKVD had been repressing prospective hostile voters, the *lishentsy*, up to this point. It's important to realize, however, that we have no evidence that this was so. After the October 1937 CC Plenum it would have made no sense to do this.

There is no question that the CC members in February-March and in June 1937 opposed competitive elections to the soviets. This opposition is firmly documented. But repression – meaning mass murder and mass imprisonment – of hostile prospective voters to prevent a hostile takeover of the soviets makes no sense after October 1937, for after that there would be no contested elections.

In January 1938 Pavel Postyshev was sharply criticized, then removed from the Politburo, then in February from the CC, then arrested, and ultimately tried and convicted, for being a part of the Rightist conspiracy. According to the evidence now available Postyshev was indeed repressing Party members, especially Party officials. The main resolution of the January 1938 CC Plenum was aimed at unwarranted mass expulsion of Party members by higher Party officials.

Judging from the scanty documentation we have today, Postyshev was also terrorizing many others. According to one account of this evidence, between June 1937 and January 1938, when he was removed from office, Postyshev had 34,540 persons prosecuted for criminal offenses and about 5000 shot. Stalin said that Postyshev was shooting the whole Party leadership and destroying the Party on thin grounds or on no grounds at all. [2]

Postyshev's actions in Kuibyshev are consistent with his being both a part of the Rightist conspiracy and engaging in the kind of massive, illegal executions of innocent people on the flimsiest of grounds or on no grounds at all, that Frinovskii and Ezhov agreed were part of their NKVD conspiracy. Postyshev agreed to this charge to which he confessed in April 1938 and, evidently, was the reason Molotov and Voroshilov went to see him in prison to learn from his own lips that he was guilty.

Postyshev may have told the truth. Or he may have been forced by Ezhov to confess, after he was already exposed at the January 1938 CC Plenum.

Therefore it appears that at least some CC members were repressing Party members. It was after the failure of the Tukhachevskii conspiracy that, according to Ezhov, he began his massive repressions of innocent Soviet citizens, of whom Party members must have been a very small proportion.

---

[2] See "The January 1938 CC Plenum," pp. 99 ff. above.

Chapter 18: Conclusion

The only conclusion supported by the evidence is that the mass murders of many tens of thousands of Soviet citizens was the result of a conspiracy by Nikolai Ezhov, People's Commissar of the NKVD.

In the introduction we stated the three principal questions about the "Ezhovshchina" or "Great Terror" as follows:

1) Did hundreds of thousands of innocent victims meet their deaths?

2) Was Stalin responsible for these murders, as is usually claimed?

3) If – as the evidence demands us to conclude -- Stalin was innocent and was part of putting a stop to this crime against humanity, how could he and his colleagues have been oblivious to what was happening for so long?

The answers to the first two questions are yes, and no, respectively.

The answer to question three is more complex. The evidence shows that it took a long time for the Stalin leadership to realize what was going on, on a national level. In the meantime Ezhov was supplying Stalin and the leadership with voluminous documentation of conspiracies, many of which were falsified but some of which were genuine.

What happened was a kind of mirror image of the Big Lie technique. As Hitler explained it in *Mein Kampf*, the "big lie" is a falsehood that is so big, so important, that most people will be unwilling to think anyone would try to get away with unless it were true. Paradoxically, it thereby becomes difficult to believe that it isn't true and is therefore accepted.

There were at least three reasons that the Stalin leadership took so long to realize what was happening before they put a stop to it and executed those responsible.

* There were genuine conspiracies behind which Ezhov et al. were able to hide their unhidden trials and executions (out in the open and well reported to the CC), as justified attempts to end the conspiracies.

* The Stalin leadership was occupied with many very complex tasks at the time – including preparing for a coming war that they well recognized was mainly designed to crush their revolution, needing to re-educate an entire population to become class-conscious co-operators rather than the selfish individualists that capitalism had trained people to be for centuries, the need to organize and rule over a vast geographical area (the largest country in the world in area). Because of these complex multiple tasks, all of which were absolute necessities, the Stalin leadership was forced to delegate tasks, around the immense country, to people they thought they could trust.

* The natural difficulty of believing the hints that came in, slowly at first, that something awful was actually occurring at the hands of their trusted delegates. This must have been particularly hard since such stories could have been inspired precisely by the very enemies they hoped to eliminate.

Terminology

"Great Terror" is a misleading name, but not because no one was terrorized. Certainly many people were. It is misnamed because Robert Conquest invented the term "Great Terror" to mean "*Stalin's* Purge of the '30s," and it was no such thing. Ezhov picked a great many of his victims at random, a process that must have sparked great fear. But this was not the Soviet government, not "Stalin." The mass murders, the only events that could have spread "terror," were perpetrated not by the Soviet government but by the enemies of the Soviet government: Ezhov, his men, and some members of the political elite of the Party and state.

The Soviet population was not "ruled by terror," and the Soviet population generally was not "terrorized." The term "great terror" is false in the way in which Conquest used it and in the way it continues to be used in the biased field of Soviet history. The falsehood is located not in the assertion that there was terror but in the claim as to who the terrorists were.

Ezhov's mass repressions were a continuation of the conspiracies described at the three Moscow Trials and the Tukhachevskii Affair. Ezhov had long been a Rightist. He initiated his own NKVD conspiracy – the mass murders – after the military conspiracy had been discovered and, in the main, destroyed.

Ezhov acted together with at least one of the military conspirators, Marshal Egorov. He fooled Stalin and the Soviet leadership with false reports, many of which have survived.

When, finally, news of massive illegal repressions reached a certain level Stalin and Politburo reacted. First they removed Frinovskii as Ezhov's deputy and put Lavrentii Beria in his place. Later Ezhov was persuaded, or forced, to resign. The repressions immediately stopped. Investigation began to disclose the enormity of Ezhov's crimes.

During 1939 Ezhov and many of his men were arrested and made confessions. Ezhov and Frinovskii gave the general outlines, and much of the detail, of their massive crimes. The small number of these confessions that have been published constitute an important body of evidence. Source criticism shows that there are no objective grounds to dismiss them.

A great many innocent persons had been murdered. From 1939 into the war years Beria, as head of the NKVD, and the Soviet Procuracy reviewed hundreds of thousands of cases and released hundreds of thousands of persons whom they judged had been wrongly imprisoned.

At the same time they continued to investigate, uncover, and punish persons who really were involved in anti-Soviet conspiracies. Real conspiracies did exist. Ezhov's and Frinovskii's confessions make it clear that not everyone repressed under Iagoda and Ezhov was innocent. These investigations continued into the war years.

Tokaev and Svetlanin testify to the fact that some conspirators were never identified.

This is the only version of the mass repressions that can be supported by the evidence. It is confirmed by the convergence of a great many individual pieces of evidence. The "mainstream" explanation for the Ezhovshchina is that Stalin intended and planned it. But there is not now, nor has there ever been, *any* evidence to support this conclusion. Rather, it flows from the *a priori* acceptance of the anti-Stalin paradigm.

It will be rejected by those who are incapable, or contemptuous, of objectivity. The false story that "Stalin the dictator" planned and carried out these massive repressions, just as he had fabricated all the alleged conspiracies is the only account tolerated by mainstream Soviet historiography. But there is no evidence to support it and a great deal of evidence that it is wrong.

Leaders of the CPSU and their researchers have long known the truth about the repressions and conspiracies. Khrushchev and his men had to lie deliberately to put forward their false version that the repressions were Stalin's doing. Gorbachev's men continued in this vein. They kept the truth a secret while inventing falsehoods to blame Stalin.

The version set forth here absolves Stalin of *guilt* for the massive repressions. This is what is unacceptable to mainstream Soviet history. But it was certainly Stalin's *responsibility*, as the principle political leader of the country, to take decisive action to stop violations of justice, have them investigated, and make sure those responsible are punished. Stalin did this. Tragically, it took him many months to fully realize what was really going on, by which time Ezhov and his men had murdered hundreds of thousands of innocent Soviet citizens.

In a 1976 review Roger Pethybridge wrote the following about the fixation on the "evil Stalin" in the historiography of the Soviet Union:

> If one considers all the well-known biographies of
> Stalin, a common feature emerges: the volumes are
> a quite accurate reflection of biographical method

> current at the end of the nineteenth and the
> beginning of the twentieth centuries, when
> historical biographies dwelt on so-called "good"
> and "bad" kings. The personality who reigned
> appeared to dominate not only the political but the
> social and economic life of his kingdom, so that by a
> sneeze or a yawn he could magically change the
> whole socioeconomic pattern of his reign. This
> method of historical biography has long been
> discounted in the treatment of authoritarian rule in
> earlier history. It has also been discarded with
> regard to the study of Nazi Germany. Unfortunately,
> it still remains as a specter from the past in the
> study of Soviet personalities in high politics.

The anti-Stalin paradigm resembles the "great man theory of history" that was already abandoned by serious historians in the 19th century. The problem was not that the Soviet system put into power a paranoid or psychopathically murderous person as, following Khrushchev, so many anticommunist and Trotskyist histories claim. Rather, the problem – the failure – was systemic.

Most Bolsheviks, like most Soviet citizens, were honorable, hardworking, and devoted to the cause of socialism and communism. But a small number of them were not honorable and devoted, or began that way but were corrupted, so that immense injustices were perpetrated and enormous harm was done.

The Bolshevik Party promoted people to positions of power who used that power to commit massive crimes. German, Japanese, and other foreign intelligence services made use of some of these persons. But the basic corruption came from within: not only from intelligence agents of capitalist countries – though they certainly played a role – but from the retention, or insufficiently thorough rejection, of the ideas and values of exploitative, capitalist society.

Unresolved Issues

There are some issues that are not clear. One of them is the question of the relationship between Stalin's push for contested elections and the Right-Trotskyist conspiracy involving First Secretaries and the NKVD.

Stalin's push for competitive elections was defeated, and competitive elections taken off the table, just before the October, 1937 CC Plenum. Therefore mass repression cannot have been aimed at *lishentsy*, at least not after mid-October 1937.

One hypothesis is that Stalin wished to break up the "family groups" of leaders and their followers who dominated the Bolshevik Party local leaderships, and therefore had them killed on some pretext or other. It is certainly true that almost all of the First Secretaries elected at the XVII Party Congress in 1934 were convicted and executed as part of the Right-Trotskyist conspiracy.

But the evidence now available suggests that, on the contrary, it was these powerful local Party leaders, the "Soviet prefects," who wanted to get rid of Stalin! Getting rid of Stalin and those loyal to him, and putting into power a leadership with a Rightist economic and political agenda, was the goal of the Rights in the bloc.

The other purported explanation of the mass repressions is that Stalin himself wanted to suppress – kill or imprison – any potential "Fifth Column" in a way with Germany or Japan. As it happens, this is true – but not in the way it has been understood by mainstream anticommunist historiography. This "fifth column explanation' is false in that the exaggerated application of death sentences to hundreds of thousands of innocent persons was not Stalin's doing. Rather, Ezhov did this under the guise of ridding the nation of its actual and undisputed "Fifth Column" of conspirators.

We know that these conspiracies existed and we know the mechanism by which Ezhov concealed from Stalin and the central leadership just what he was up to. There is no evidence whatever to support the version that Ezhov's mass murders were Stalin's doing. This version contradicts all the evidence we do have. It survives because it "saves" the anti-Stalin paradigm.

Resolution

The evidence we now have supports two hypotheses. First, that many First Secretaries and other Party leaders were involved in the Right-Trotskyist conspiracy. Second, that some of them were also directly involved with Ezhov's NKVD conspiracy. Jansen and Petrov cite evidence that Robert Eikhe was involved with Ezhov's conspiracy. Eikhe is also mentioned by Frinovskii in his statement to Beria of April 11, 1939.

Pavel Postyshev, who confessed to being a member of the Right-Trotskyist conspiracy, was involved in massive repressions against innocent people, both Party members and others, in Kuibyshev. Ezhov and Frinovskii did exactly this. It appears likely that Postyshev too was involved in both conspiracies.

Ezhov's conspiracy was a spinoff of the Right-Trotskyist conspiracy. Ezhov testified that he began his massive executions after the executions of Tukhachevskii and other leaders of the military conspiracy. This is consistent with what we know of Eikhe's and Postyshev's mass repressions. It was a very dangerous moment for the Soviet state and Ezhov took advantage of it.

From the beginning the Right-Trotskyist conspiracy was a bloc of different oppositional groups, originating as anti-Stalin factions, with somewhat different programs and different leaderships. The Trotskyists did not trust the Rights, nor did the Rights, like Iagoda and Bukharin, trust the Trotskyists or agree with Trotsky in some respects. Tukhachevskii was aligned with both but saw himself as the eventual leader of the state. Ezhov too aimed to be the next leader of the Soviet Union. Each faction in the bloc was willing to sacrifice the others to save themselves.

Defeatism and assassination were common threads in all the conspiracies. The former oppositionists, and many former Stalin supporters too, could not believe that the USSR would succeed. Either the pressures of crash industrialization and collectivization would cause the Stalin government to collapse, perhaps in widespread rebellion, or a combination of capitalist states would attack and defeat the Red Army. Such fears, admixed with personal ambition, sparked and fueled the conspiracies.

Objections

The principal objection to this explanation is that it does not find Stalin guilty of them. It will be claimed that the confession statements on which it is based are false, fabrications. Rejection of this evidence is essential if the genuine nature of the anti-Soviet conspiracies is to be denied.

But this is wrong. We have tested the confessions in the Moscow Trials and those of Frinovskii and Ezhov by source criticism. There is no legitimate basis at all to reject them as fabrications. The real reason they are rejected or ignored is that they are incompatible with the anti-Stalin paradigm.

It is sometimes claimed that Ezhov was tortured. But there no evidence that Ezhov or Frinovskii were tortured.

It appears that the Right-Trotskyist conspirators had a kind of code of *omertà*: a practice of not identifying other members of the conspiracy whose identity was not yet known to the NKVD, even if it meant their own execution. Stalin drew this conclusion from Piatakov's behavior and expressed it at the December 1936 CC Plenum.

> ...we questioned about 50 people, at least. They really turned Piatakov inside out. It turns out that he's a monster of a person! So why did he agree to be the public prosecutor? Why did he agree to shoot his comrades himself? It turns out that they have a rule like this: If your fellow Trotskyist is arrested and has begun to give up the names of others, he must be destroyed. You can see what kind of hellish joke this comes to. Believe after this in the sincerity of former oppositionists! We can't take former oppositionists at their word even when they volunteer to shoot their friends with their own hands.[1]

---

[1] Extract from J.V. Stalin's presentation (Dec. 1936 CC Plenum). *Voprosy Istorii* 1, 1995, 9-11. At https://msuweb.montclair.edu/~furrg/research/stalinonoppsvi11995.html

It appears that Stalin was correct. As Frinovskii points out, Bukharin, Radek, Iagoda and others did not identify Ezhov as part of the conspiracy even though they went to their deaths. Zinoviev and Kamenev did not identify Iagoda or Ezhov. At the January 1937 Moscow Trial Karl Radek swore that Tukhachevskii was a loyal Party man. He had to have known the truth: Bukharin did, and he and Radek were close.

This code did not function perfectly. Some conspirators did in fact name others. No doubt some falsely inculpated innocent persons while remaining silent about guilty ones. Others did "name names." Many conspirators were arrested and punished. But not all. Tokaev's and Svetlanin's accounts suggest that some conspirators remained unidentified. Nikita Khrushchev may have been among the conspirators who escaped detection. Such a hypothesis would help to account for his massive falsifications about Stalin and his insistence on "rehabilitating" and declaring innocent a great many persons whom we now know were in fact guilty.

Denial

This explanation for the mass repressions offered here is the one that best fits the evidence we now have. It is also utterly incompatible with mainstream Soviet historiography, which demands that Stalin be the mass murderer and Ezhov his "loyal executioner." For this reason it will be rejected by mainstream anticommunist Soviet historians and by Trotskyists. It does not fit the Procrustean bed of the anti-Stalin paradigm.

There are numerous other examples of mainstream Soviet historiography ignoring or rejecting the truth about Soviet history.

* Khrushchev's Secret Speech is virtually 100% false. This has been known for years but is never acknowledged. (Furr, *Khrushchev*)

* Sergei Kirov was indeed murdered by an underground Zinovievist gang linked through the bloc of oppositionists with Rightists, Trotskyists, and others. Since the mainstream interpretation is that no such conspiracies existed and were all fabricated by

Stalin and the NKVD, the Kirov murder continues to be falsified in spite of the evidence. (Furr, *Kirov*)

* The Katyn Massacre could not possibly have occurred in the way described by mainstream anticommunist historiography. But this massacre is far too useful as a cudgel to beat Stalin and the Soviet Union with to be abandoned simply because has been proven false. Therefore, the evidence is ignored. (Furr, *Katyn*)

* Timothy Snyder's book *Blood Lies* contains not a single true accusation against Stalin or the USSR. Yet this completely meretricious book won many prizes and continues to be widely quoted. (Furr, *Blood Lies*)

* Evidence from the Harvard Trotsky Archive proves that a political bloc of clandestine oppositionists including Rights, Trotskyists, Zinovievists, and others did in fact exist in the USSR. This proves that the Khrushchev- and Gorbachev-era "rehabilitations" are false, since they claim no such bloc existed. This fact is ignored. (Furr, *Amalgams*)

* The testimony of the defendants in the three public Moscow "Show" trials of August 1936, January 1937, and March 1938 was not fabricated or forced on them by the NKVD, the Prosecution, or Stalin. Rather, it represents what the defendants chose to say. The conspiracies alleged in the Trials really did exist. This is denied, the evidence that supports it ignored. (Furr, *Amalgams*)

A recent example of the falsification that is tolerated in the field of Soviet studies comes from the pen of the widely respected historian of Soviet science, Loren Graham. In the spring of 2016 Graham wrote in *Foreign Affairs*:

> ... thousands of biologists were sent to prison or killed for criticizing Stalin's favorite scientist [Trofim Lysenko] ...[2]

---

[2] Loren Graham, "What the Reappraisal of Soviet Russia's Top Agricultural Mastermind Says About Putin's Russia." *Foreign Affairs* http://tinyurl.com/fa-agriculture

The truth is that not a single Soviet biologist was either killed or sent to prison for criticizing Lysenko. In his 1970 book on the Lysenko affair anticommunist scholar David Joravsky has a list of all the biologists he could find out about who were "repressed" (imprisoned or executed). Joravsky was unable to show that *any* of them were repressed because of opposition to Lysenko.[3] A non-Lysenko plant biologist even won the Stalin prize in 1950. (Elina, *Lysenko*)

Lies about Stalin not only tolerated but promoted

In the academic field of Soviet history of the Stalin period false statements, so long as they are condemnatory of Stalin, are seldom criticized or refuted.

For example, Arch Getty continues to point out that "limits" are consistently mistranslated as "quotas." This is an obvious, deliberate falsification. But this flagrant mistranslation continues to be repeated by prominent scholars in the field such as Oleg Khlevniuk. Khlevniuk has consistently falsified Soviet history for decades. In another field of history – say, American history – he would have been exposed and both his credibility and his career cut short long ago.

Only in the field of Soviet history of the Stalin period is such blatant falsification virtually ignored and, in fact, rewarded, as long as it is anti-Stalin. The Soviet studies field will continue to spread falsehoods about the mass repressions of the 1930s.

Objectivity and the Truth

What is badly needed in the field of Soviet history of the Stalin period is a devotion to discovering the truth. Objectivity can only be

---

[3] David Joravsky. *The Lysenko Affair*. Harvard University Press, 1970. Appendix A. Repressed Specialists, 317-360. More recently a noted researcher and fanatic anti-Stalinist claimed to have proven that Stalin and Lysenko were responsible for the arrest and prosecution of Nikolai I. Vavilov, a famous Soviet geneticist. Despite the title of his article he is unable to cite a single shred of evidence that either Stalin or Lysenko had anything to do with Vavilov's case. See IA. G. Rokitianskii, "Stalin – initsiator, Lysenko – glavnyi podstrekatel' ubiystva akademika Ni.I. Vavilova." *Izvestiia TSKhA* 4 (2012) 150-163. Again, despite the title of this article, Vavilov was not "murdered" (ubiystvo) either.

approached by a determination to question one's own preconceived ideas, to seriously entertain the possibility that they may be
mistaken.

Like a detective working to solve a crime by finding the real cul-
prit, the historian must go where the evidence leads, and not
where he/she would prefer that it leads. And if the evidence can
only be satisfied by a hypothesis that rejects the historical models
that are popular – so be it.

In this study we have attempted to be objective. The truth is not at
all to the liking of powerful people. It nonetheless remains the
truth.

Works Cited

"'...Ni razu ne govorilos' otnositel'no terror.' Stenogramma ochnoi stavki N.I. Bukharina s V.N. Astrovym v Politburo TsK VKP(b) 13 ianvaria 1937 g." *Istochnik* No. 2, 2001, 89-110. (Bukharin-Astrov)

"Interrogations of Nikolai Ezhov, former People's Commissar for Internal Affairs," at http://msuweb.montclair.edu/~furrg/research/ezhovinterrogs.html (Ezhov, Interrogations)

"Nikolai Ezhov's Concluding Statement at Trial February 3 1940." At https://msuweb.montclair.edu/~furrg/research/ezhovlastwords.html (Ezhov, Last)

"Stenogramma ochnykh stavok v TsK VKP(b). Dekabr' 1936 goda. No. 3. Stenogramma ochnoi stavki mezhdu Piatakovym i Bukharinym v Ts.K VKP(b) ot 7 dekabria 1936 goda." *Voprosy Istorii* 4 (2003) 3-12. (Bukharin-Piatakov)

"Stenogramma ochnykh stavok v TsK VKP(b). Dekabr' 1936 goda." *Voprosy Istoriii* No. 3, 2002 3-31. (Bukharin-Kulikov)

"Transcript of the Interrogation of the Arrested Person Ezhov Nikolai Ivanovich of April 26 1939." At https://msuweb.montclair.edu/~furrg/research/ezhov042639eng.html (Ezhov 04.26.1939)

Bobrov, Vladimir L. "Taina smerti Ordzhonikidze." Originally at http://vif2ne.ru/nvz/forum/archive/238/238967.htm ; fully footnoted Russian version at http://msuweb.montclair.edu/~furr/research/bobrov-ordzhon08.html ; English translation at http://msuweb.montclair.edu/~furr/research/bobrov-ordzhon08eng.html (Bobrov, Taina)

Briukhanov, Boris Borisovich, and Shoshkov, Evgenii Nikolaevich. *Opravdaniiu ne podlezhit. Ezhov i Ezhovshchina 1936-1938 gg.* Sankt-Peterburg: OOO "Petrovskii Fond" 1998. (Briukhanov and Shoshkov)

Coox, Alvin D. "The Lesser of Two Hells: NKVD General G.S. Lyushkov's Defection to Japan, 1938-1945." *Journal of Slavic Military Studies* 11, 3 (1998) 145-186. (Coox, Lesser 1)

Elina, Ol'ga Iurev'na. "Mezhdu nauchnoi teoriei i sel'skokhoziastvennoi praktikoi. Selektsionery i Lysenko (1948-1955 gg.). In M. Khainemann and E.I. Kolchinskii, eds., *Za 'Zeleznym zanavesom': mify I realii sovetskoi naukia.* St. Petersburg, 2002, 376-392. (Elina, Lysenko)

Ellman, Michael. "The Soviet 1937–1938 Provincial Show Trials Revisited." *Europe-Asia Studies* 55:8 (2003) 1305-1321. (Ellman, Trials)

Frinovskii, M.P. ."..ot arestovannogo FRINOVSKOGO M.P. ZAIAV-LENIE." Lubianka 3 33-60. Russian original at https://msuweb.montclair.edu/~furrg/research/frinovskyru.html English translation at https://msuweb.montclair.edu/~furrg/research/frinovskyeng.html (Frinovskii)

Furr, Grover and Vladimir L. Bobrov. "Stephen Cohen's Biography of Bukharin: A Study in the Falsehood of Khrushchev-Era 'Revelations'." In *Cultural Logic* 2010. At http://clogic.eserver.org/2010/Furr.pdf (Furr & Bobrov, Cohen)

Furr, Grover. *Blood Lies. The Evidence that Every Accusation Against Joseph Stalin and the Soviet Union in Timothy Snyder's Bloodlands Is False.* New York: Red Star Publications, 2014. (Furr, Blood Lies)

Furr, Grover. *Khrushchev Lied: The Evidence That Every "Revelation" of Stalin's (and Beria's) Crimes in Nikita Khrushchev's Infamous "Secret Speech" to the 20th Party Congress of the Communist Party of the Soviet Union on February 25, 1956, is Provably False.* Kettering, OH: Erythrós Press & Media LLC, 2011. (Furr, Khrushchev)

Furr, Grover. "Stalin and the Struggle for Democratic Reform" (two parts) in *Cultural Logic* (2005). At http://clogic.eserver.org/2005/furr.html and http://clogic.eserver.org/2005/furr2.html

Furr, Grover. "The 'Official Version' of the Katyn Massacre Dis-proven? Discoveries at a German Mass Murder Site in Ukraine." *Socialism and Democracy* 27, 2 (2013), 96-129. (Furr, Katyn)

Furr, Grover. *The Murder of Sergei Kirov. History, Scholarship and the Anti-Stalin Paradigm.* Kettering, OH: Erythrós Press and Media, LLC, 2013. (Furr, Kirov)

Furr, Grover. *Trotsky's "Amalgams": Trotsky's Lies, The Moscow Trials As Evidence, The Dewey Commission. Trotsky's Conspiracies of the 1930s, Volume One.* Kettering, OH: Erythrós Press & Media, LLC, 2015. (Furr, Amalgams)

Getty, J. Arch, *Practicing Stalinism. Bolsheviks, Boyars, and the Persistence of Tradition.* Yale University Press, 2013. (Getty, Practicing)

Getty, J. Arch. "Excesses are not permitted.: Mass Terror and Stalinist Governance in the Late 1930s." *The Russian Review* Vol.61 (January 2002) 113-138. (Getty, Excesses)

Getty, J. Arch. "Pre-election Fever: The Origins of the 1937 Mass Operations." In Harris, Anatomy 216-235. (Getty, Fever)

Getty, J. Arch. "The Rise and Fall of a Party First Secretary: Vainov of Iaroslavl'." In Harris, *Anatomy* 66-84. (Getty, Rise)

Getty, J. Arch. Origins of the Great Purges. The Soviet Communist Party Reconsidered, 1933-1938. New York and Cambridge: Cambridge University Press, 1985. (Getty, Origins)

Getty, J. Arch and Oleg V. Naumov, *The Road to Terror. Stalin and the Self-Destruction of the Bolsheviks, 1932-1939.* New Haven: Yale University Press, 1999. (Getty & Naumov)

Goldman, Wendy Z. *Inventing the Enemy: Denunciation and Terror in Stalin's Russia.* Cambridge University Press, 2011. (Goldman, Inventing)

Goldman, Wendy Z. *Terror and Democracy in the Age of Stalin. The Social Dynamics of Repression.* Cambridge University Press, 2007. (Goldman, Terror)

Gur'ianov, A. Ie. "Obzor sovetskikh repressivnykh kampanii protiv poliakov i pol'skikh grazhdan," in A. V. Lipatov and I. O. Shaitanov, eds., *Poliaki i russkie: Vzaimoponimanie i vzaimoneponimanie*, Moscow: Indrik, 2000, 199-207.

Gur'ianov, A. Ie. "Obzor sovetskikh repressivnykh kampanii protiv poliakov i pol'skikh grazhdan," in Massovye repressii protiv poliakov. Memorial Society. At http://www.memo.ru/history/polacy/vved/index.htm [This is a brief summary of Gur'ianov's longer article above.]

Harris, James, ed. *The Anatomy of Terror. Political Violence Under Stalin*. Oxford University Press, 2013. (Harris, Anatomy)

Ilic, Melanie, ed. *Stalin's Terror Revisited*. Palgrave-Macmillan, 2006. (Ilic, Terror)

Jansen, Mark, and Nikita Petrov. *Stalin's Loyal Executioner. People's Commissar Nikolai Ezhov 1895-1940*. Stanford: Hoover Institution Press, 2002. (Jansen & Petrov)

Khaustov, Vladimir, and Lennart Samuel'son. *Stalin, NKVD, i Repressii 1936-1938 gg.* "Istoriia Stalinizma" series. Moscow: ROSSPEN, 2009. (Khaustov-Samuel'son)

Lubianka. Sovetskaia elita na stalinskoi golgofe 1937-1938. Dokumenty. Moscow: Mezhdunarodnyi Fond "Demokratiia." 2011. (Lubianka Golgofa)

Lubianka. Stalin i Glavnoe Upravlenie Gosbezopasnosti NKVD. 1937-1938. Moscow: "Materik," 2004. (Lubianka 1937-1938)

Lubianka. Stalin i NKVD-NKGB-GUKR "Smersh." 1939 – mart 1946. Moscow: MDF, 2006 (Lubianka 1939-1946)

Merritt, Steven E. *The Great Purges in the Soviet Far East, 1937-1938*. Ph.D. dissertation U. Cal Riverside, 2000.

Morris, James. "The Polish Terror: Spy Mania and Ethnic Cleansing in the Great Terror." *Europe-Asia Studies* 56, 5 (July 2004), 751-766.

Naumov, Leonid A. *Stalin i NKVD*. Moscow: Novyi Khronograf, 2010. (Naumov, Stalin)

Nikita Petrov, Mark Iansen. *"Stalinskii pitomets" – Nikolai Ezhov*. Moscow: ROSSPEN, 2008 (Petrov & Iansen)

Okhotin, N.G. and A.B. Roginskii, "'Bol'shoi Terror' 1937-1938. Kratkaia Khronika." At http://www.memo.ru/history/y1937/hronika1936_1939/xronik a.html ("'The Great Terror': 1937-1938. A Short Chronology.") (Khronika)

Pavliukov, Aleksei. *Ezhov. Biografia*. Moscow: Zakharov, 2007.

Pethybridge, Roger. Review of Ronald Hingley, *Joseph Stalin: Man and Legend*. *Slavic Review* 35, 1 (March 1976), 135-137.

Petrov, Nikita V. and A. B. Roginsksii, "'Pol'skaia operatsiia' NKVD 1937-1938 gg." in A. Ie. Gur'ianov, ed., *Repressii protiv poliakov i pol'skikh grazhdan*, Moscow: Zven'ia, 1997, 22-43.

N.V. Petrov, K.V. Skorkin. *Kto rukovodil NKVD. 1934-1941. Spra- vochnik*. Moscow: Zven'ia, 1999. (Petrov, Kto). Also online at http://old.memo.ru/history/NKVD/kto/index.htm

Polianskii, Aleksei. *Ezhov. Istoriia «zheleznogo» stalinskogo narkoma*. Moscow: «Veche», «Aria-AiF», 2001. (Pavliukov, Ezhov)

Reabilitatsiia: Kak Eto Bylo. Mart 1953 – Fevral' 1956 gg. Dokumenty Prezidiuma TsK KPSS i Drugie Materialy. Moskva: Mezhdunarodniy Fond "Demokratiia," 2000. (RKEB 1)

Report of Court Proceedings in the Case of the Anti-Soviet "Bloc of Rights and Trotskyites" Heard Before the Military Collegium of the Supreme Court of the U.S.S.R. Moscow, March 2-13, 1938...Verbatim Report. Moscow: People's Commissariat of Justice of the U.S.S.R., 1938. (1938 Trial)

Shearer, David R., and Vladimir Khaustov. *Stalin and the Lubianka. A Documentary History of the Political Police and Security Organs in the Soviet Union, 1922–1953*. Yale University Press, 2015 (Shearer & Khaustov)

Shentalinskii, Vitalii. *Donos na Sokrata*. Moscow: Formika-S, 2001 (Shentalinskii, Donos)

Soima, Vassili. *Zapreshchennyi Stalin, Chast' 1*. Moscow: OLMA- PRESS, 2001.

Stalin, Joseph V.. "On the Draft of the Constitution of the USSR." In Russian: *Collected Works*, vol. 14. At <

http://grachev62.narod.ru/stalin/t14/t14_44.htm>; in English, in J.V. Stalin, *Problems of Leninism*. Foreign Languages Press, Peking 1976, 795-834, at <http://www.marx2mao.com/Stalin/SC36.html>. (Stalin, Draft)

Stalin, Joseph V.. "Vystuplenie I.V. Stalina na Rasshirennom Zasedanii Voennogo Soveta pri Narkome Oborony," *Istochnik* 3 (1994), 72-88. A slightly different version is in Lubianka 1937-1938, No. 92 202-209. (Stalin, Vystuplenie)

Stalin, Joseph V.. "Zakluchitel'noe slovo na plenume tsentral'nogo komiteta VKP(b) 5 marta 1937 goda (stenograficheskii variant)." At <http://grachev62.narod.ru/stalin/t14/t14_44.htm>. (Stalin, Zakliuchitel'noe)

Stalin, Joseph V.. *The Stalin-Howard Interview*. NY: International Publishers, 1936. (Stalin-Howard) In Russian at <http://grachev62.narod.ru/stalin/t14/t14_33.htm>

Suturin, A. *Delo kraevogo masshtaba*. Khabarovsk: Khabarovskoe knizhnoe izdalte'stvo, 1991. (Suturin, Delo)

Thurston.Robert W. *Life and Terror in Stalin's Russia, 1934–1941*. Yale University Press; 1998. (Thurston, Life)

Tragediia Sovetskoi Derevni Tom 5 chast' 2. Ed. V. Danilov et al. Moscow: ROSSPEN 2006. (TSD 5,2)

Vasiliev, Valerii. "The Great Terror in the Ukraine, 1936–38." In Ilic, *Stalin's Terror Revisited*, 140-162. (Vasiliev, Terror)

Wheatcroft, Stephen G. "Agency and Terror: Evdokimov and Mass Killing in Stalin's Great Terror." *Australian Journal of Politics and History* 53:1 (2007) 20-43. (Wheatcroft, Agency)

Wheatcroft, Stephen G. "From Team-Stalin to Degenerate Tyranny." In E.A. Rees, ed., *The Nature of Stalin's Dictatorship. The Politburo, 1924-1953.* Basingstoke: Palgrave Macmillan, 2004, 79-107.

Zhukov, Iurii. "Zhupel Stalina." („The Stalin Boogeyman") *Komsomolskaia Pravda* November 5, 6, 12-14, 16, 19-21, 2002. (Zhukov, Zhupel)

Zhukov, Iurii. *Inoi Stalin. Politicheskie reformy v SSSR v 1933-1937 gg.* Moscow:"Vagrius," 2003. (Zhukov, Inoi)

Zhukov, Iurii, "Repressii i Konstitutsiia SSSR 1936 goda." *Voprosy Istorii.* 2002, No. 1, pp. 3-26. (Zhukov, Repressii)

Zhukov, Iurii, "Zhupel Stalina," *Komsomolskaya Pravda*, November 5, 6, 12, 13, 14, 15, 19, 20, 2002. Also widely available on the Internet, e.g. at <http://www.x-libri.ru/elib/smi_958/>.

Zhukov, Iurii, *Tainy Kremlia: Stalin, Molotov, Beria, Malenkov.* Moscow: Terra-Knizhnyy Klub, 2000. (Zhukov, Tainy)

The Stalin-Howard Interview. New York: International Publishers, 1936. (Stalin-Howard)

Index.

15270111R00146

Printed in Great Britain
by Amazon